S0-APN-828

TEST TAKING STARS
(Strategies To Achieve Raised Scores)

INTRODUCTION

Test Taking is a tool to assist your students in learning to take tests. Research shows that students who are acquainted with the scoring format of standardized tests score higher on these tests. Students also score higher when they practice and encounter the pressures of timed tests. The concepts presented for practice are typically found on standardized tests for students at the fourth-grade level. *The scores on these activities are indicators of a student's ability to take tests, not necessarily to master the concepts used for practice.* Students who practice with STARS will grow comfortable with the variety of processes needed to improve test scores.

ORGANIZATION

Each of the seven units focuses on specific test-taking areas in content: Word Analysis; Vocabulary; Spelling and Language; Study Skills; Reading Comprehension; Math Concepts and Computation; and Problem Solving. Practice lessons introduce students to the typical formats they can expect to see. These pages identify strategy tips for improving accuracy and speed. At the bottom of each lesson, students are encouraged to evaluate their performance. Again, the goal is to improve students' ability to perform well on tests. At the end of each unit, a practice test is included. Students have the opportunity to apply the strategies they learned in the lessons and to demonstrate their abilities to successfully complete a test.

USE

STARS is designed for independent use by students who have had instruction in the specific skills covered in these workbooks. Copies of the activities can be given to individuals, pairs of students, or small groups for completion. They can also be used as a center activity.

To begin, determine the implementation which fits your students' needs and your classroom structure. The following plan suggests a format for this implementation:

1. Explain the purpose of the worksheets to your class.

2. Review the mechanics of how you want students to work with the exercises. Do you want to check the practice lessons before they begin the practice tests? Do you want to discuss the samples in each lesson?

3. Determine how the timed tests will be monitored. If students are to do the timed tests on their own, what timing instrument should they use? Do you want to administer the timed tests to the whole class or to a group that has successfully completed a series of practice lessons?

4. Introduce students to the process and to the purpose of the activities. Make copies of the **DOs and DON'Ts** for test taking, and review with students.

5. Discuss the component of tracking progress. Give a copy of the *STARS Record Chart* to each student. Identify a place for the progress chart to be maintained, i.e. in a folder, inside the

students' notebooks, etc. (You may want to keep these progress charts to include in students' portfolios.)

6. <u>Assure</u> students that all of the material is for practice purposes only. It is to help them do better on tests.

7. <u>Do</u> a practice activity together.

ADDITIONAL NOTES

1. <u>Time Limits</u>. The time limits for each practice test are suggested limits. You may choose to ignore them or to set limits which you think are more appropriate for your students.

2. <u>Parent Communication</u>. Sign the **Letter to Parents**. Duplicate and send home with the students. Decide if you want to keep the activity pages and practice tests in portfolios for conferencing, or if you want students to take them home as they complete them.

3. <u>Bulletin Board</u>. Display the **DOs and DON'Ts** for test taking in your classroom for quick reference.

4. <u>Student Evaluation</u>. In the student evaluation section of the practice activities, encourage students to identify interferences that affect their performance on tests, such as conflicts with peers, lack of sleep, inadequate breakfast, etc.

5. <u>Have fun</u>. Reducing the pressure associated with test taking can be fun as well as meaningful for you and your students. Look forward to positive results and to improved test scores!

Dear Parent,

Sometime during this school year, our class will be taking mandated standardized tests. To increase your child's skills in test taking, we will be working with sample tests to give him or her the tools to perform well. Test taking can be stressful. By working together to prepare the students, we can reduce their stress level.

From time to time, I may send home lesson practice sheets. To best help your child, please consider the following suggestions:

- Provide a quiet place to work.
- Go over the directions and the sample exercises together.
- Review the Strategy Tips.
- Reassure your child that the practice sheets are not a "real" test.
- Encourage your child to do his or her best.
- Record the amount of time it takes to complete the lesson.
- Check the lesson when it is complete.
- Go over the answers and note improvements as well as problems.

Help your child maintain a positive attitude about taking a standardized test. Let your child know that each test provides an opportunity to shine. If your child expresses anxiety about taking a test or completing these lessons, help him or her understand what causes the stress. Then, talk about ways to eliminate anxiety. Above all, enjoy this time you spend with your child. He or she will feel your support, and test scores will improve as success in test taking is experienced.

Thank you for your help!

Cordially,

Dear Student:

Your teacher has announced that you will be taking some tests during the school year. You're wondering how well you'll do. Many people feel anxious when they have to take a test. Suddenly they can't think, and they're sure that they have forgotten everything they ever knew. There are ways to avoid those feelings. You will be doing practice lessons and tests that will help you prepare for taking tests. In addition to the DOs and DON'Ts, you'll find strategy tips for taking specific tests on the practice pages.

As you work with practice lessons, remember the following:
- Read the directions carefully.
- Look for key words that tell exactly what you have to do.
- Read and think about the strategy tips for each lesson before beginning to work.
- Study the sample questions and the reasons given for the correct answer.
- Read each test question carefully.
- Stop working whenever you come to the word *STOP*.
- Check your answers with the teacher.
- Record your score on the special STARS chart.
- Treat the practice tests as though they are real tests.

Your practice will help you improve your test taking. Have fun as you develop new skills!

Name_____ Date _____

STARS DOs AND DON'Ts FOR TEST TAKING

DO:
- listen to or read all the directions.
- read all the samples and STRATEGY TIPS for each lesson before you begin.
- look over the entire test or section before you begin.
- stay calm, concentrate on the test, and clear your mind of things that have nothing to do with the test.
- read all the answer choices before choosing the one that you think is best.
- make sure the number you fill in on the answer sheet matches the question number on the test page.
- trust your first instinct when answering each question.
- answer the easy questions first, then go back and work on the ones you aren't sure about.
- take all the time you are allowed.

DON'T:
- look ahead to another question until you complete the one you're working on.
- spend too much time on one question.
- rush.
- worry if others finish while you are still working.
- change an answer unless you are really sure it should be changed.

DO your very best!

6

Student _____

	number of questions	number right	date
Unit I: **Word Analysis**			
lesson 1	6	_____	_____
lesson 2	12	_____	_____
lesson 3	6	_____	_____
Practice Test 1	18	_____	_____
Unit II: **Vocabulary**			
lesson 1	6	_____	_____
lesson 2	6	_____	_____
lesson 3	6	_____	_____
lesson 4	6	_____	_____
lesson 5	12	_____	_____
Practice Test 2	22	_____	_____
Unit III: Spelling and Language			
lesson 1	8	_____	_____
lesson 2	5	_____	_____
lesson 3	6	_____	_____
lesson 4	4	_____	_____
lesson 5	5	_____	_____
lesson 6	6	_____	_____
lesson 7	4	_____	_____
Practice Test 3	27	_____	_____
Unit IV: **Study Skills**			
lesson 1	7	_____	_____
lesson 2	6	_____	_____
lesson 3	10	_____	_____
lesson 4	10	_____	_____
Practice Test 4	24	_____	_____

	number of questions	number right	date
Unit V: Reading Comprehension			
lesson 1	4	_____	_____
lesson 2	5	_____	_____
lesson 3	12	_____	_____
lesson 4	12	_____	_____
Practice Test 5	18	_____	_____
Unit VI: **Math Concepts and Computation**			
lesson 1	14	_____	_____
lesson 2	14	_____	_____
lesson 3	9	_____	_____
lesson 4	4	_____	_____
lesson 5	3	_____	_____
lesson 6	9	_____	_____
Practice Test 6	16	_____	_____
Unit VII: **Problem Solving**			
lesson 1	2	_____	_____
lesson 2	8	_____	_____
Practice Test 7	8	_____	_____

Name_____ Date _____

Practice Test ____ Answer Sheet

1. Ⓐ Ⓑ Ⓒ Ⓓ Ⓔ		21. Ⓐ Ⓑ Ⓒ Ⓓ Ⓔ
2. Ⓐ Ⓑ Ⓒ Ⓓ Ⓔ		22. Ⓐ Ⓑ Ⓒ Ⓓ Ⓔ
3. Ⓐ Ⓑ Ⓒ Ⓓ Ⓔ		23. Ⓐ Ⓑ Ⓒ Ⓓ Ⓔ
4. Ⓐ Ⓑ Ⓒ Ⓓ Ⓔ		24. Ⓐ Ⓑ Ⓒ Ⓓ Ⓔ
5. Ⓐ Ⓑ Ⓒ Ⓓ Ⓔ		25. Ⓐ Ⓑ Ⓒ Ⓓ Ⓔ
6. Ⓐ Ⓑ Ⓒ Ⓓ Ⓔ		26. Ⓐ Ⓑ Ⓒ Ⓓ Ⓔ
7. Ⓐ Ⓑ Ⓒ Ⓓ Ⓔ		27. Ⓐ Ⓑ Ⓒ Ⓓ Ⓔ
8. Ⓐ Ⓑ Ⓒ Ⓓ Ⓔ		28. Ⓐ Ⓑ Ⓒ Ⓓ Ⓔ
9. Ⓐ Ⓑ Ⓒ Ⓓ Ⓔ		29. Ⓐ Ⓑ Ⓒ Ⓓ Ⓔ
10. Ⓐ Ⓑ Ⓒ Ⓓ Ⓔ		30. Ⓐ Ⓑ Ⓒ Ⓓ Ⓔ
11. Ⓐ Ⓑ Ⓒ Ⓓ Ⓔ		31. Ⓐ Ⓑ Ⓒ Ⓓ Ⓔ
12. Ⓐ Ⓑ Ⓒ Ⓓ Ⓔ		32. Ⓐ Ⓑ Ⓒ Ⓓ Ⓔ
13. Ⓐ Ⓑ Ⓒ Ⓓ Ⓔ		33. Ⓐ Ⓑ Ⓒ Ⓓ Ⓔ
14. Ⓐ Ⓑ Ⓒ Ⓓ Ⓔ		34. Ⓐ Ⓑ Ⓒ Ⓓ Ⓔ
15. Ⓐ Ⓑ Ⓒ Ⓓ Ⓔ		35. Ⓐ Ⓑ Ⓒ Ⓓ Ⓔ
16. Ⓐ Ⓑ Ⓒ Ⓓ Ⓔ		36. Ⓐ Ⓑ Ⓒ Ⓓ Ⓔ
17. Ⓐ Ⓑ Ⓒ Ⓓ Ⓔ		37. Ⓐ Ⓑ Ⓒ Ⓓ Ⓔ
18. Ⓐ Ⓑ Ⓒ Ⓓ Ⓔ		38. Ⓐ Ⓑ Ⓒ Ⓓ Ⓔ
19. Ⓐ Ⓑ Ⓒ Ⓓ Ⓔ		39. Ⓐ Ⓑ Ⓒ Ⓓ Ⓔ
20. Ⓐ Ⓑ Ⓒ Ⓓ Ⓔ		40. Ⓐ Ⓑ Ⓒ Ⓓ Ⓔ

Test Taking 4, SV 6773-5

UNIT I: WORD ANALYSIS

Lesson 1: Comparing with adjec

DIRECTIONS ▶ Darken the circle for the form of the adjectiv
each sentence.

💡 **STRATEGY TIPS**

1. Remember that most adjectives have three forms. The **positive degree** (small), the **comparative degree** (smaller), and the **superlative degree** (smallest).
2. Read each sentence. Decide which comparative adjective is correct.

Sample:

My math homework is
_____ than my sister's.

Ⓐ hardest   Ⓒ harder
Ⓑ hard   Ⓓ more hard

✦ **ANSWER**

The correct answer is *C. harder*. The sentence compares only two things, your homework and your sister's homework. When two things are compared, use the comparative degree.

✏️ **NOW TRY THESE**

1. Keisha is the _____ girl in her class.

   Ⓐ taller   Ⓒ most tall
   Ⓑ tall   Ⓓ tallest

2. Rhode Island is the _____ state in the U.S.

   Ⓐ more small   Ⓒ small
   Ⓑ smallest   Ⓓ smaller

3. Shiho is the _____ dancer I ever saw.

   Ⓐ gracefullest   Ⓒ most graceful
   Ⓑ gracefuller   Ⓓ more graceful

4. That was the _____ meal I ever ate!

   Ⓐ bestest   Ⓒ more best
   Ⓑ best   Ⓓ most best

5. Yesterday was the _____ day of the year.

   Ⓐ warmest   Ⓒ most warm
   Ⓑ warmer   Ⓓ warm

6. Mason did the _____ high jump ever.

   Ⓐ good   Ⓒ best
   Ⓑ goodest   Ⓓ bestest

🛑 **STOP**

Your time: _____   Number right: _____

On this lesson I did _____ because _____.

Date _____

2: Working with prefixes and suffixes

one

TIONS ▶ Darken the circle of the prefix that changes the meaning of the root word to the new definition.

STRATEGY TIPS
1. Think about the meaning of the root word.
2. Decide which prefix will change the root word to match the definition.

Sample:
Which prefix changes the meaning of <u>view</u> to <u>view again</u>?

Ⓐ dis   Ⓒ re
Ⓑ un   Ⓓ non

ANSWER

The correct answer is *C. re.* The prefix *re* means again. When you review something, you look at it again.

NOW TRY THESE

1. Which prefix changes the meaning of <u>honest</u> to <u>not honest</u>?
   Ⓐ re   Ⓒ pre
   Ⓑ dis   Ⓓ ex

2. Which prefix changes the meaning of <u>competent</u> to <u>not competent</u>?
   Ⓐ ex   Ⓒ re
   Ⓑ in   Ⓓ pre

3. Which prefix changes the meaning of <u>used</u> to <u>not used</u>?
   Ⓐ pre   Ⓒ re
   Ⓑ con   Ⓓ un

4. Which prefix makes the word <u>count</u> mean <u>count wrong</u>?
   Ⓐ non   Ⓒ re
   Ⓑ mis   Ⓓ ex

5. Which prefix added to <u>weekly</u> makes it mean <u>twice weekly</u>?
   Ⓐ dis   Ⓒ in
   Ⓑ bi   Ⓓ en

6. Which prefix would you use to make the word <u>tell</u> mean <u>tell again</u>?
   Ⓐ ex   Ⓒ un
   Ⓑ non   Ⓓ re

GO ON TO NEXT PAGE

Name_____   Date _____

Lesson 2: Working with prefixes and suffixes
Part two

DIRECTIONS ▶ Darken the circle of the suffix that changes the root word's part of speech.

 **STRATEGY TIPS**

1. Study the root word. Decide whether it is a noun, verb, or adjective.
2. Think about what each of these parts of speech means.
3. Decide which suffix would change the root word to a different part of speech.

Sample:

Which suffix changes the verb teach to a noun?

Ⓐ ed   Ⓒ er
Ⓑ ly   Ⓓ ful

ANSWER

The correct answer is *C. er*. The word *teacher* is a noun about a person who teaches.

NOW TRY THESE

7. Which suffix changes the adjective thick to a verb?

   Ⓐ ness   Ⓒ en
   Ⓑ ful   Ⓓ ly

8. Which suffix changes the noun danger to an adjective?

   Ⓐ ous   Ⓒ ful
   Ⓑ ly   Ⓓ able

9. Which suffix changes the verb act to a noun?

   Ⓐ ish   Ⓒ ful
   Ⓑ ing   Ⓓ or

10. Which suffix changes the noun joy to an adjective?

    Ⓐ ed   Ⓒ ful
    Ⓑ er   Ⓓ ness

11. Which suffix changes the verb help to an adjective?

    Ⓐ less   Ⓒ er
    Ⓑ ing   Ⓓ en

12. Which suffix changes the verb attend to a noun?

    Ⓐ ing   Ⓒ ance
    Ⓑ or   Ⓓ ion

STOP

Your time: _____   Number right: _____

On this lesson I did _____ because _____

_____ .

Name_____ Date _____

Lesson 3: Understanding word origins

DIRECTIONS ▶ Darken the circle for the word we use today that is close to the meaning of the original word.

 **STRATEGY TIPS**

1. Read the meaning of the original word.
2. Find the word we use today that is closest in meaning to the original word.

Sample:

Which word probably comes from the Old English word <u>launde</u>, meaning land?

  Ⓐ large   Ⓒ lean
  Ⓑ lake   Ⓓ lawn

ANSWER

The correct answer is *D. lawn.* A lawn is grown on land. *Large*, *lake*, and *lean* do not have meanings close to *land*.

NOW TRY THESE

1. Which word probably comes from the Latin word <u>caput</u>, meaning head?

  Ⓐ carpet   Ⓒ caper
  Ⓑ cabbage   Ⓓ castle

2. Which word probably comes from the French word <u>moton</u>, meaning meat from sheep?

  Ⓐ mutton   Ⓒ matter
  Ⓑ motion   Ⓓ mobile

3. Which word came from the name <u>Louis Pasteur</u>, a French scientist who sterilized liquids?

  Ⓐ pastor   Ⓒ pasture
  Ⓑ pasteurize   Ⓓ pastime

4. Which word probably came from the Old English word <u>windeye</u>, meaning an opening in the wind?

  Ⓐ winter   Ⓒ winding
  Ⓑ window   Ⓓ winnow

5. Which word probably comes from the Latin word <u>addere</u>, meaning to put together?

  Ⓐ adder   Ⓒ add
  Ⓑ addle   Ⓓ admit

6. Which word probably comes from the Spanish word <u>cacao</u>, a bean from a chocolate tree?

  Ⓐ cola   Ⓒ coconut
  Ⓑ cocoa   Ⓓ cook

STOP

Your time: _____ Number right: _____

On this lesson I did _____ because _____

_____.

Name_____   Date _____

PRACTICE TEST 1
Part 1

Directions: For questions 1–5, choose the form of the adjective that best fits each sentence. Record your answer on the answer sheet.

Sample: That's the _____ bridge I have ever seen.

A long   C longed
B longer   D longest

Answer: The correct answer is *D. longest*. This is a superlative comparison.

---

1. **Junius said that the swimming pool at his school is _____ than the pool in the park.**

    A deeper   C deepest
    B deepen   D deep

2. **My second grade teacher was the _____ teacher I ever had.**

    A nice   C most nice
    B nicest   D nicer

3. **Red, yellow, and green are usually very _____ colors.**

    A brighter   C bright
    B brighten   D brightest

4. **Carlos liked that book _____ of all.**

    A better   C best
    B goodest   D bestest

5. **Winston has _____ model cars than his big brother.**

    A many   C mostest
    B more   D most

Name_____   Date _____

Part 2

Directions: For questions 6–8, choose the word or words that give the best meaning of the underlined prefix. Record your answer on the answer sheet.

Sample: You should <u>re</u>view your notes for the social studies test.

A not   C again
B always   D with

Answer: The correct answer is *C. again.*

6. We are learning about <u>tri</u>angles in our math class.

   A three   B two   C over   D made of

7. Ms. Harper <u>mis</u>understood the directions.

   A after   B not   C away   D again

8. Leola went to the <u>pre</u>view of a scary movie.

   A near   B over   C before   D under

Part 3

Directions: For questions 9–14, choose the letter of the prefix or suffix that changes the meaning of the root word to the new definition. Record your answer on the answer sheet.

Sample: Which prefix changes the meaning of <u>happy</u> to not happy?

A re   C dis
B un   D im

Answer: The correct answer is *B. un.*

9. Which suffix makes <u>mountain</u> mean an area with more than one mountain?

   A ness   C ful
   B ly   D ous

10. Which prefix makes <u>draw</u> mean to draw again?

    A re   C im
    B un   D pre

Name_____   Date _____

11. Which prefix makes <u>lock</u> mean to open?

   A non   **C** bi
   B re   **D** un

12. Which prefix makes <u>legal</u> mean not legal?

   A ex   **C** re
   B il   **D** in

13. Which suffix makes <u>kind</u> mean the quality of being kind?

   A ful   **C** ness
   B less   **D** able

14. Which suffix makes <u>child</u> mean like a child?

   A ible   **C** ous
   B ish   **D** less

Part 4

Directions: For questions 15–18, choose the word we use today that is close to the meaning of the original word. Record your answer on the answer sheet.

Sample: Which word probably comes from the old French word <u>feit</u>, meaning to trust?

   A fate   **C** faith
   B fair   **D** fear

Answer: The correct answer is *C. faith*.

15. Which flower was named for French botanist Pierre <u>Magnol</u>?

   A petunia   **C** primrose
   B marigold   **D** magnolia

16. Which word probably came from the Latin <u>angere</u>, meaning to strangle?

   A ankle   **C** anger
   B angle   **D** anxious

17. Which word probably came from the Old English word <u>gaman</u>, meaning amusement?

   A gap   **C** gamut
   B gaze   **D** game

18. Which word probably comes from the Middle English word <u>disporten</u>, meaning to amuse oneself?

   A spring   **C** spool
   B spray   **D** sport

Suggested Time Limit: 12 minutes   Your time: _____
Check your work if you have time. Wait for instructions from your teacher.

Name_____ Date _____

UNIT II: VOCABULARY

Lesson 1: Finding synonyms

DIRECTIONS ▶ Darken the circle for the word that has the <u>same</u> or <u>almost the same</u> meaning as the underlined word.

💡 **STRATEGY TIPS**

1. Read each sentence carefully.
2. Try each answer choice in place of the underlined word.
3. Decide which word means the same or almost the same as the underlined word.

Sample:

Connie will <u>purchase</u> the cookies for our party.

Ⓐ find   Ⓒ bake
Ⓑ get   Ⓓ buy

ANSWER

The correct answer is *D. buy*. All of the choices could describe what Connie will do about the cookies for the party, but only *buy* means the same as *purchase*.

✏️ **NOW TRY THESE**

1. The baby <u>crawled</u> on the rug.

  Ⓐ slid   Ⓒ sat
  Ⓑ crept   Ⓓ slept

2. There was a <u>heap</u> of books on the floor.

  Ⓐ pile   Ⓒ box
  Ⓑ bag   Ⓓ number

3. Morgan's job was to <u>greet</u> the visitors.

  Ⓐ call   Ⓒ find
  Ⓑ welcome Ⓓ reach

4. I saw a <u>fabulous</u> movie last week.

  Ⓐ silly   Ⓒ great
  Ⓑ funny   Ⓓ lovely

5. The caterpillar was <u>transformed</u> into a moth.

  Ⓐ crossed   Ⓒ sprouted
  Ⓑ changed Ⓓ enlarged

6. Tony signed a <u>contract</u> to complete a social studies unit.

  Ⓐ letter   Ⓒ message
  Ⓑ report   Ⓓ agreement

🛑 STOP

Your time: _____ Number right: _____

On this lesson I did _____ because _____ .

Name_____ Date _____

Lesson 2: Finding antonyms

DIRECTIONS ▶ Darken the circle for the word that means the opposite of the underlined word in the sentence.

STRATEGY TIPS

1. Try each word in the sentence.
2. Compare it to the underlined word.
3. Which word means the opposite of the underlined word?

Sample:

Which picture did you <u>choose</u>?

  Ⓐ like   Ⓒ reject

  Ⓑ notice   Ⓓ prefer

ANSWER

The correct answer is *C. reject*. All of the choices make sense in the sentence, but *reject* is the only word that means the opposite of *choose*.

NOW TRY THESE

1. Wynton always does <u>thoughtful</u> things for others.

  Ⓐ happy   Ⓒ selfish

  Ⓑ silly   Ⓓ honest

2. I like <u>firm</u> chocolate chip cookies, don't you?

  Ⓐ crusty   Ⓒ chewy

  Ⓑ soft   Ⓓ tasty

3. A rubber band can <u>expand</u> to fit a package.

  Ⓐ contract Ⓒ inflate

  Ⓑ stretch   Ⓓ twist

4. Food was <u>scarce</u> on the long journey.

  Ⓐ delicious Ⓒ abundant

  Ⓑ growing   Ⓓ frozen

5. She wore <u>sturdy</u> shoes on the mountain hike.

  Ⓐ flimsy   Ⓒ comfortable

  Ⓑ leather   Ⓓ heavy

6. Should we <u>extend</u> our vacation by one week?

  Ⓐ lengthen Ⓒ shorten

  Ⓑ continue Ⓓ enjoy

STOP

Your time: _____   Number right: _____

On this lesson I did _____ because _____

_____.

17

Test Taking 4, SV 6773-5

Name_____   Date _____

Lesson 3: Finding analogies

DIRECTIONS ▶ Darken the circle for the word that finishes the analogy.

STRATEGY TIPS

1. Think about what the first pair of words in the sentence have in common.
2. Find the word that has the same thing in common with the question word.

Sample:

House is to people as nest is to _____ .

Ⓐ tree   Ⓒ birds
Ⓑ cage   Ⓓ roof

ANSWER

The correct answer is *C. birds*. What the words have in common is that they describe different kinds of homes. Houses are for people. Nests are for birds.

NOW TRY THESE

1. Fingers are to hands as toes are to _____ .

   Ⓐ shoes   Ⓒ gloves
   Ⓑ feet   Ⓓ thumbs

2. Glad is to bad as big is to _____ .

   Ⓐ pig   Ⓒ small
   Ⓑ had   Ⓓ large

3. Road is to car as track is to _____ .

   Ⓐ truck   Ⓒ plane
   Ⓑ bus   Ⓓ train

4. Pull is to push as sit is to _____ .

   Ⓐ walk   Ⓒ hop
   Ⓑ stand   Ⓓ tug

5. Baby is to crib as adult is to _____ .

   Ⓐ table   Ⓒ chair
   Ⓑ bed   Ⓓ carriage

6. Beach is to swim as restaurant is to _____ .

   Ⓐ sand   Ⓒ eat
   Ⓑ menu   Ⓓ read

STOP

Your time: _____

Number right: _____

On this lesson I did _____ because _____

_____ .

Name_____   Date _____

Lesson 4: Using words with multiple meanings

DIRECTIONS ▶ Darken the circle for the word that has both underlined meanings.

STRATEGY TIPS

1. Only one word will fit both definitions.
2. Try each word in place of each group of underlined words.
3. Decide whether the word you chose fits both definitions.

Sample:

car shoe or wear out

Ⓐ wheels   Ⓒ tire
Ⓑ spokes   Ⓓ drive

ANSWER

The correct answer is *C. tire.*
A shoe on a car is called a *tire.*
When you wear out, you *tire.*

NOW TRY THESE

1. an insect or travel through air

   Ⓐ gnat   Ⓒ mosquito
   Ⓑ plane   Ⓓ fly

2. not heavy or not dark

   Ⓐ dim   Ⓒ sunny
   Ⓑ light   Ⓓ weight

3. have fun with friends or a stage show

   Ⓐ laugh   Ⓒ play
   Ⓑ song   Ⓓ opera

4. a name for a stone or move back and forth

   Ⓐ pebble   Ⓒ roll
   Ⓑ marble   Ⓓ rock

5. an extra tire or a bowling score

   Ⓐ rim   Ⓒ spare
   Ⓑ strike   Ⓓ lean

6. to lose fur or feathers or a small building

   Ⓐ shed   Ⓒ clip
   Ⓑ shear   Ⓓ hut

STOP

Your time: _____

Number right: _____

On this lesson I did _____ because _____

_____

_____.

Name_____   Date _____

Lesson 5: Using context clues

DIRECTIONS ▶ Darken the circle of the word that best completes each sentence.

 **STRATEGY TIPS**

1. Read the sentence. Then decide what the sentence is about.
2. Think about which word would best fit into the sentence.

Sample:

Do you enjoy reading and solving _____ ?

Ⓐ books   Ⓒ maps
Ⓑ stories   Ⓓ riddles

ANSWER

The correct answer is *D. riddles.* You can read books, stories, and maps, but you can't solve them. Riddles can be read and solved.

NOW TRY THESE

1. At the end of the year all of the winners were _____ at a large banquet.

   Ⓐ stung   Ⓒ sitting
   Ⓑ honored   Ⓓ stolen

2. We were _____ by the strange noises we heard.

   Ⓐ startled   Ⓒ strained
   Ⓑ served   Ⓓ skilled

3. My father made a _____ for a room at a motel with a swimming pool.

   Ⓐ splash   Ⓒ sensation
   Ⓑ dinner   Ⓓ reservation

4. Native Americans thought that buffaloes were very _____ animals. The meat was used for food, and the hides were used for clothing and tents.

   Ⓐ large   Ⓒ useful
   Ⓑ strange   Ⓓ wild

5. Most people in China do not own cars. They use _____ instead.

   Ⓐ sleds   Ⓒ tools
   Ⓑ bicycles   Ⓓ magazines

6. Many people enjoy going to _____ to see the art exhibits.

   Ⓐ movies   Ⓒ theaters
   Ⓑ stores   Ⓓ museums

GO ON TO NEXT PAGE

20   Test Taking 4, SV 6773-5

Name_____   Date _____

Unit 2, lesson 5, page 2

7. Long ago some people thought bathing was _____ . They thought they might get sick.

   Ⓐ foolish   Ⓒ funny
   Ⓑ unhealthy   Ⓓ dirty

8. They hired a ____ to take pictures of the wedding.

   Ⓐ caterer   Ⓒ musician
   Ⓑ florist   Ⓓ photographer

9. You should always store meat in the refrigerator to prevent it from _____ .

   Ⓐ cooking   Ⓒ spoiling
   Ⓑ roasting   Ⓓ melting

10. People who _____ about the things they own can be very boring.

    Ⓐ boast   Ⓒ laugh
    Ⓑ cry   Ⓓ stare

11. The speaker made an important _____ to the people in the audience.

    Ⓐ record   Ⓒ announcement
    Ⓑ notice   Ⓓ discovery

12. Because there is a shortage of supplies, there is a two-pencil _____ for each student.

    Ⓐ charge   Ⓒ limit
    Ⓑ score   Ⓓ cost

STOP

Your time: _____

Number right: _____

On this lesson I did _____ because _____ .

I think it would help me to _____

_____

_____ .

Name_____   Date _____

PRACTICE TEST 2
Part 1

Directions: For questions 1–6, choose the word that means the same or almost the same as the underlined word in the sentence. Record your answer on the answer sheet.

Sample: Did you <u>enjoy</u> going to the ball game?

      A try   **C** stop
      B like   **D** hate

Answer: The correct answer is *B. like*. When you enjoy something, you like it.

---

1. **Gerald's room always looks nice and <u>neat</u>.**

   A sunny   **C** clear
   B new   **D** tidy

2. **There is a design in the <u>center</u> of the rug.**

   A corner   **C** border
   B middle   **D** fiber

3. **There was a <u>smudge</u> of soil on the farmer's face.**

   A spot   **C** scratch
   B piece   **D** group

4. **Everyone was asked to <u>contribute</u> food for the party.**

   A buy   **C** donate
   B sell   **D** cook

5. **Hank <u>inspected</u> the model car before he bought it.**

   A touched **C** examined
   B tried   **D** started

6. **The lake water looked <u>calm</u>.**

   A choppy   **C** rough
   B still   **D** wavy

GO ON TO NEXT PAGE

Name_____   Date _____

Part 2

Directions: For questions 7–10, choose the word that is the opposite of the underlined word in the sentence. Record your answer on the answer sheet.

Sample: Be sure to check your bill to see if it is <u>correct</u>.

A right   C torn
B accurate   D wrong

Answer: The correct answer is *D. wrong*. Wrong is the only one of the four choices which is the opposite of correct.

---

7. **The building has lots of <u>gloomy</u> areas.**

   A sunny   C chilly
   B dark   D useless

8. **Please <u>leave</u> with me.**

   A roam   C stay
   B float   D ramble

9. **Some young children like to play with <u>imaginary</u> friends.**

   A many   C thin
   B real   D happy

10. **He thinks the Atlantic Ocean is a <u>vast</u> body of water.**

    A salty   C small
    B deep   D great

Part 3

Directions: For questions 11–14, choose the word that best completes the sentence. Record your answer on the answer sheet.

Sample: <u>Hard</u> is to <u>soft</u> as <u>clear</u> is to _____.

A lumpy   C glass
B cloudy   D window

Answer: The correct answer is *B. cloudy*. Cloudy is the opposite of clear just as soft is the opposite of hard.

---

11. **<u>Blades</u> are to <u>ice skates</u> as <u>wheels</u> are to _____.**

    A tennis   C sleds
    B soccer   D in-line skates

12. **<u>Last</u> is to <u>loser</u> as <u>first</u> is to _____.**

    A runner   C winner
    B racer   D skipper

13. **<u>Students</u> are to <u>school</u> as <u>athletes</u> are to _____.**

    A buildings   C basketball
    B teams   D scores

14. **<u>Throat</u> is to <u>coat</u> as <u>linger</u> is to _____.**

    A opera   C record
    B finger   D guitar

GO ON TO NEXT PAGE

Name_____   Date _____

Part 4

Directions: For questions 15–18, choose the word that has both underlined meanings. Record your answer on the answer sheet.

Sample: **<u>a color</u> or <u>a fruit</u>**

     A pear   **B** orange   **C** purple   **D** apple

Answer: The correct answer is *B. orange*. It is the only word that is a fruit and a color.

---

15. **<u>call loudly</u> or <u>rain turned to ice</u>**

  A shout   **C** hail
  B sleet   **D** snow

16. **<u>place for keeping money</u> or <u>side of a river</u>**

  A safe   **C** stream
  B bank   **D** bridge

17. **<u>to mend a hole</u> or <u>a piece of ground</u>**

  A sew   **C** patch
  B repair   **D** dirt

18. **<u>plan of a story</u> or <u>a garden area</u>**

  A riddle   **C** ending
  B bed   **D** plot

Part 5

Directions: For questions 19–22, choose the word that best completes each sentence. Record your answer on the answer sheet.

Sample: We were _____ it was going to rain, so we canceled the picnic.

    A happy   **B** positive   **C** unsure   **D** glad

Answer: The correct answer is *B. positive*. The other words would not be a reason to cancel a picnic.

---

19. High waterfalls usually drop from very _____ cliffs.

  A wide   **C** shallow
  B steep   **D** simple

20. The platypus is _____ at ease on land or in water. It can swim to catch food, but it sleeps in a burrow on the shore.

  A equally   **C** never
  B sometimes   **D** hardly

21. Sometimes big stars _____ and leave tiny bits behind.

  A freeze   **C** explode
  B fall   **D** dance

22. The hornbill is a bird that lives in _____ in the forests of Africa and Asia.

  A cities   **C** treetops
  B cocoons   **D** deserts

Suggested Time Limit: 18 minutes. Your time: _____

Name_____   Date _____

UNIT III: SPELLING AND LANGUAGE

Lesson 1: Spelling correctly
Part one

DIRECTIONS ▶ Darken the circle for the underlined word that is misspelled in each sentence. If all the words are spelled correctly, darken the circle for <u>No mistake</u>.

STRATEGY TIPS
1. Read the sentence carefully.
2. Decide which of the underlined words you are sure are spelled correctly.
3. See if you can identify the misspelled word from your reading knowledge.

Sample:

 Kayla is <u>hopeing</u> to <u>wear</u> her new dress <u>tomorrow</u>. <u>No mistake</u>.
 (A)   (B)   (C)   (D)

ANSWER

The correct answer is *A. hopeing*. All of the other underlined words are spelled correctly. *Hopeing* should be spelled *h-o-p-i-n-g*. Drop the *e* when adding *ing*.

NOW TRY THESE

1. The <u>fourth</u> grade <u>childrin</u> are going on a <u>field</u> trip next week. <u>No mistake</u>.
   (A)   (B)   (C)   (D)

2. <u>Everyone</u> is <u>busy</u> working on a <u>special</u> project. <u>No mistake</u>.
   (A)   (B)   (C)   (D)

3. Hugo <u>bought</u> a box of <u>pencils</u> for <u>fourty</u> cents. <u>No mistake</u>.
   (A)   (B)   (C)   (D)

4. We <u>allmost</u> lost <u>directions</u> for making the <u>model</u> plane. <u>No mistake</u>.
   (A)   (B)   (C)   (D)

Name_____   Date _____

Lesson 1: Spelling correctly
Part two

DIRECTIONS ▶ Darken the circle for the word that is spelled correctly.

 **STRATEGY TIPS**

1. Decide which words are not spelled correctly.
2. Then look for the word that looks like one you have seen in your reading.

Sample:

What did you _____
to the party?

  Ⓐ weer   Ⓒ were
  Ⓑ wear   Ⓓ wier

ANSWER

The correct answer is *B. wear*.
The other words may look or
sound like *wear* but w-e-a-r is
the only correct spelling.

NOW TRY THESE

5. We are going to _____ how
   to use a computer.

  Ⓐ lern   Ⓒ lirne
  Ⓑ terne   Ⓓ learn

6. There was _____ cake for
   twenty children.

  Ⓐ enough   Ⓒ enugh
  Ⓑ enuogh   Ⓓ enouff

7. I am _____ going to read
   that book.

  Ⓐ definitly   Ⓒ defenitly
  Ⓑ definitely Ⓓ defenitely

8. We _____ watch TV after
   dinner.

  Ⓐ usally   Ⓒ uasully
  Ⓑ usualy   Ⓓ usually

STOP

Your time: _____

Number right: _____

On this lesson I did _____ because _____

_____ .

I think it would help me to _____

_____ .

Name_____   Date _____

Lesson 2: Using correct capitalization

DIRECTIONS ▶ Darken the circle for the part of the sentence that needs a capital letter. Darken the circle for *D. none* if no capital letter is needed.

 **STRATEGY TIPS**

1. Look at each part of the sentence carefully.
2. Proper nouns, names of weekdays and months, titles of books, titles of films, the word *I*, and the first word in a sentence or quotation should be capitalized.

Sample:

Roy said,	"let's go outside	to play."	none
Ⓐ	Ⓑ	Ⓒ	Ⓓ

⚡ **ANSWER**

The correct answer is *B. "let's go outside.* The word *let's* should start with a capital letter because it is the first word in a quotation.

✏ **NOW TRY THESE**

1.	Sunday is	my favorite	day of the week.	none
	Ⓐ	Ⓑ	Ⓒ	Ⓓ

2.	Spring	will begin	on march 21.	none
	Ⓐ	Ⓑ	Ⓒ	Ⓓ

3.	Juan and i	like to collect	comic books.	none
	Ⓐ	Ⓑ	Ⓒ	Ⓓ

4.	Next year	we will start	to study spanish.	none
	Ⓐ	Ⓑ	Ⓒ	Ⓓ

5.	Robert l. stevenson	is the author of	Treasure Island.	none
	Ⓐ	Ⓑ	Ⓒ	Ⓓ

STOP

Your time: _____   Number right: _____

On this lesson I did _____ because _____ .

Name_____   Date _____

Lesson 3: Using correct punctuation

DIRECTIONS ▶ Darken the circle for the punctuation mark that makes the sentence correct. Darken the circle for *D. none* if no other punctuation is needed.

STRATEGY TIPS

1. Read each sentence.
2. Think about the punctuation rules you use when you write.

Sample:

Did you enjoy that book

(A) "   (C) ?

(B) !   (D) none

ANSWER

The correct answer is *C. ?*. Always use a question mark when asking a question.

NOW TRY THESE

1. We bought notebooks pens, and paper clips at the stationery store.

   (A) .   (C) ,

   (B) ;   (D) none

2. Don't slam the door!

   (A) :   (C) ?

   (B) "   (D) none

3. Colin said, This is my favorite toy."

   (A) "   (C) '

   (B) !   (D) none

4. The American flag is red, white, and blue.

   (A) !   (C) ;

   (B) "   (D) none

5. When are you leaving

   (A) ?   (C) "

   (B) .   (D) none

6. Disney World is in Orlando Florida.

   (A) !   (C) ,

   (B) ?   (D) none

STOP

Your time: _____

Number right: _____

On this lesson I did _____ because _____

_____ .

I think it would help me to _____

_____ .

Name_____ Date _____

Lesson 4: Using correct capitalization and punctuation

DIRECTIONS ▶ Darken the circle for the sentence that has correct capitalization and punctuation. Choose *D. correct as is* if you think all of the sentences have the correct capitalization and punctuation.

STRATEGY TIPS Pretend that you are the author of these sentences. Use the rules of correct capitalization and punctuation to choose your answer.

Sample:

Ⓐ We're going to athens, Greece next summer.
Ⓑ Today is the first day of winter.
Ⓒ the first tuplips of spring are in bloom!
Ⓓ correct as is

ANSWER

The correct answer is *B. Today is the first day of winter.* All of the other sentences have either a capitalization or punctuation error.

NOW TRY THESE

1. Ⓐ Mr. Herman and ms. Jones are partners
   Ⓑ I'm going to order a burger fries, and a milkshake!
   Ⓒ Joanna said, "Let's bake cookies this afternoon."
   Ⓓ correct as is

2. Ⓐ The train stops at Grand Avenue.
   Ⓑ It's a nice day, isn't it?
   Ⓒ Stop that noise!
   Ⓓ correct as is

3. Ⓐ My uncle jim is coming to visit, tomorrow.
   Ⓑ We'll need glue, glitter, and crepe paper to make the decorations.
   Ⓒ July and august are the hottest months of the year
   Ⓓ correct as is

4. Ⓐ We arrived in Tucson on March 4 1997.
   Ⓑ Dear aunt Betsy, Thank you for the birthday gift.
   Ⓒ No, Nadji cannot go to the park.
   Ⓓ correct as is

STOP

Your time: _____ Number right: _____

On this lesson I did _____ because _____

_____.

Name _____   Date _____

Lesson 5: Understanding grammar

DIRECTIONS ▶ Darken the circle for the underlined word in the sentence that answers the question about nouns, verbs, or adjectives. Darken the circle for *D. none* if none of the words answer the question.

💡 **STRATEGY TIPS**

Think about these as you read each sentence:
1. A noun names a person, place, or thing.
2. A verb tells about an action.
3. An adjective tells something about a noun.

ANSWER

The correct answer is *A. pretty. Pretty* is an adjective because it describes the cat.

Sample:

Which of the underlined words is an adjective?
The <u>pretty</u> cat <u>sat</u> on the window <u>sill</u>. none
     Ⓐ   Ⓑ   Ⓒ   Ⓓ

✏️ **NOW TRY THESE**

1. Which of the underlined words is a verb?
   <u>It</u> <u>snowed</u> last <u>night</u>. none
   Ⓐ Ⓑ   Ⓒ   Ⓓ

2. Which of the underlined words is an adjective?
   <u>Garret</u> built a <u>huge</u> sand <u>castle</u>. none
   Ⓐ   Ⓑ   Ⓒ   Ⓓ

3. Which of the underlined words is an adjective?
   The <u>firefighter</u> <u>arrived</u> at the <u>mayor's</u> house. none
     Ⓐ   Ⓑ   Ⓒ   Ⓓ

4. Which of the underlined words is a noun?
   Mr. Ling <u>says</u> that <u>Amy</u> is a <u>good</u> student. none
       Ⓐ   Ⓑ   Ⓒ   Ⓓ

5. Which of the underlined words is a verb?
   <u>Rosie</u> always walks <u>home</u> from <u>school</u>. none
   Ⓐ   Ⓑ   Ⓒ   Ⓓ

🛑 STOP

Your time: _____   Number right: _____

On this lesson I did _____ because _____.

Name_____   Date _____

Lesson 6: Choosing correct usage

DIRECTIONS ▶ Darken the circle for the word or words that make the sentence correct.

💡 **STRATEGY TIPS**

1. Read each sentence carefully.
2. Try each answer choice in the sentence.
3. Decide which one makes the most sense.

Sample:

Perry shared his candy with
Ethan and _____ .

Ⓐ me   Ⓒ she
Ⓑ I   Ⓓ we

⚡ ANSWER

The correct answer is *A. me.* Think how the sentence would sound if you took away the words *Ethan and. Me* would be the correct answer.

✏️ **NOW TRY THESE**

1. We'll _____ the house at noon.

   Ⓐ leaves   Ⓒ leave
   Ⓑ leaving   Ⓓ left

2. I _____ piano lessons for two years.

   Ⓐ taked   Ⓒ taking
   Ⓑ took   Ⓓ takes

3. Our family _____ on a long trip.

   Ⓐ had went   Ⓒ went
   Ⓑ have went   Ⓓ goes

4. Theresa _____ hummed the words to the song.

   Ⓐ softly   Ⓒ softest
   Ⓑ soft   Ⓓ softer

5. The librarian read _____ a very funny book.

   Ⓐ we   Ⓒ myself
   Ⓑ ourselves   Ⓓ us

6. Is _____ the one who found the ring?

   Ⓐ she   Ⓒ him
   Ⓑ her   Ⓓ his

🛑 **STOP**

Your time: _____

Number right: _____

On this lesson I did _____ because _____

_____ .

Name_____   Date _____

Lesson 7: Combining sentences

 **DIRECTIONS** ▶ Darken the letter of the sentence that best combines the two underlined sentences.

STRATEGY TIPS
1. When combining sentences, keep the meaning of both sentences.
2. Say the new sentence to yourself. Does it have the same meaning as the two sentences that were combined?

Sample:

Gary won the freestyle race.

He placed second in the breast stroke race.

Ⓐ Gary won the freestyle race and Gary placed second in the breast stroke race.
Ⓑ Gary won the freestyle race and placed second in the breast stroke race.
Ⓒ Gary won the freestyle and placed second in the breast stroke races.
Ⓓ Gary, he won the freestyle race and came in second in the breast stroke race.

 ANSWER

The correct answer is *B*. Sentence B keeps the meaning of both sentences and uses correct English.

NOW TRY THESE

1. We trudged through the snow.

The snow was deep.

Ⓐ We trudged through the snow and it was deep.
Ⓑ The snow was deep and we trudged through it.
Ⓒ We trudged through the deep snow.
Ⓓ It was hard to trudge through the deep snow.

2. There are many statues in the park.

The statues are of heroes of our country.

Ⓐ There are many statues of heroes in the park.
Ⓑ There are many statues of our country's heroes in the park.
Ⓒ The park has many statues.
Ⓓ Our country's heroes are shown in the park.

 GO ON TO NEXT PAGE

Name_____   Date _____

Unit 3, lesson 7, page 2

3. Jan Lyons told us about the new
   software.

   Jan Lyons is a computer expert.

   Ⓐ Jan Lyons told us about the new
      software because she is a
      computer expert.
   Ⓑ Jan Lyons, a computer expert,
      told us about the new software.
   Ⓒ Jan Lyons is a computer expert
      and she told us about the new
      software.
   Ⓓ Jan Lyons is a computer expert
      about the new software.

4. The concert had to be postponed.

   The soloist was sick.

   Ⓐ Since the soloist was sick, the
      concert had to be postponed.
   Ⓑ The soloist was sick, and they
      postponed the concert.
   Ⓒ The concert had to be
      postponed, so the soloist was
      sick.
   Ⓓ Because the concert had to be
      postponed, the soloist was sick.

STOP

Your time: _____

Number right: _____

On this lesson I did _____ because _____

_____ .

I think it would help me to _____

_____

_____ .

Name_____   Date _____

PRACTICE TEST 3

Part 1

Directions: For questions 1–3, choose the underlined word that is <u>misspelled</u> in each sentence. If all the words are spelled correctly, choose <u>*D. No mistake.*</u> Record your answer on the answer sheet.

Sample: Robin is <u>comeing</u> to my <u>house</u> after school <u>tomorrow</u>. <u>No mistake</u>
              A   **B**   **C**   **D**

Answer: The correct answer is *A. comeing.* The word *comeing* should be spelled *c-o-m-i-n-g.*

1. My puppy <u>always</u> <u>trys</u> to chase <u>squirrels</u>. <u>No mistake</u>
                      A   **B**   **C**   **D**

2. Next <u>week</u> our class will <u>visit</u> a famous <u>auther</u>. <u>No mistake</u>
              A   **B**   **C**   **D**

3. We were all <u>surprised</u> when our <u>neghbor</u> won the <u>medal</u>. <u>No mistake</u>
                      A   **B**   **C**   **D**

Part 2

Directions: For questions 4–6, choose the word that is spelled correctly. Record your answer on the answer sheet.

Sample: **Our seats for the play are in the _____ row.**

              A eigth   B aith   C eighth   D eight

Answer: The correct answer is *C. eighth.*

4. **The mall is _____ the main highway.**

    A across   B accross   C accros   D acrost

5. **My sister took the test for her driver's _____ .**

    A lisens   B liscence   C licence   D license

6. **The mayor of our _____ will be honored for her good work.**

    A villege   B village   C villige   D vilage

GO ON TO NEXT PAGE

Name_____   Date _____

Part 3

Directions: For questions 7–9, choose the part of the sentence that needs a capital letter. Choose *D. none* if no capital is needed. Record your answer on the answer sheet.

Sample:

Roy's best friend	Andy lives on	Linden boulevard.	none
A	**B**	**C**	**D**

Answer: The correct answer is *C. Linden boulevard. Boulevard* should be capitalized because it names a specific place.

7.
Tyler will play	a piece by Mozart	at the recital.	none
A	**B**	**C**	**D**

8.
Did you see	*Beauty and the beast*	on television?	none
A	**B**	**C**	**D**

9.
Our school	has a Science Fair	every march.	none
A	**B**	**C**	**D**

Part 4

Directions: For questions 10–12, choose the punctuation mark that would make the sentence correct. Choose *D. none* if no other punctuation is needed. Record your answer on the answer sheet.

Sample: **Mom said, I need to go to the supermarket later today."**

A ?   **C** ,

B "   **D** none

Answer: The correct answer is *B. ".*

---

10. April 7 1997 is the date of our school picnic.

A ,   **B** .   **C** ;   **D** none

11. They plan to serve pretzels potato chips, and popcorn at the party.

A !   **B** ?   **C** ,   **D** none

Name_____   Date _____

12. Watch out for that cactus plant

    A !   **B** "   **C** ?   **D** none

Part 5

Directions: For questions 13–15, choose the sentence that has the correct capitalization and punctuation. Record your answer on the answer sheet.

      Sample: **A** Let's take a walk, said Iris.
                            B Sam has a lovely Singing Voice.
                            C May I get you a glass of milk?
                            D When I saw the new baby, I cried?

Answer: The correct answer is *C. May I get you a glass of milk?* All of the other sentences have either a capitalization or punctuation error.

---

13. **A** "What a beautiful painting!" exclaimed Hugo.
     B Our plane took off from Kennedy airport
     C Yes Sara, is my best friend
     D Will you help me set the table.

14. **A** Mr. chian told us about his trip.
     B Vincent's cousin, lives in California.
     C Everyone thought i was Julio's brother.
     D Uncle Gary goes camping every September.

15. **A** My homeroom teacher is mr. McGraw.
     B The fireworks at Victoria Park are really special!
     C Would you like to ski in Vale Colorado?
     D Yes, Rosie has, a lovely singing voice.

GO ON TO NEXT PAGE

Name_____   Date _____

Part 6

Directions: For questions 16–19, choose the underlined word in the sentence that answers the question about nouns, verbs, or adjectives. Choose *D. none* if none of the words answer the question. Record your answer on the answer sheet.

Sample: **Which of the underlined words is an adjective?**

My <u>cousin</u> Cary <u>bought</u> a <u>green</u> sweater.   <u>none</u>
    A   B   C   D

Answer: The correct answer is *C. green*. Green describes the sweater.

---

16. **Which of the underlined words is a verb?**

    Can <u>you</u> <u>jump</u> over the <u>rope</u>? <u>none</u>
        A   B   C   D

17. **Which of the underlined words is an adjective?**

    <u>Who</u> <u>rang</u> the <u>doorbell</u>? <u>none</u>
     A   B   C   D

18. **Which of the underlined words is a noun?**

    Kyle's <u>mother</u> is a <u>very</u> <u>good</u> cook. <u>none</u>
            A   B   C   D

19. **Which of the underlined words is a verb?**

    Let's play <u>with</u> that <u>big</u> orange <u>ball</u>. <u>none</u>
                A   B   C   D

GO ON TO NEXT PAGE

Name_____   Date _____

Part 7

Directions: For questions 20–24, choose the word or words that make the sentence correct. Record your answer on the answer sheet.

Sample: Tanya _____ shopping at the new mall.

     A had went
     B went
     C has went
     D goed

Answer: The correct answer is *B. went.*

---

20. He always _____ his time.

     A taken
     B taking
     C takes
     D taked

21. Listen for knocks when the motor is _____ .

     A run
     B ran
     C runned
     D running

22. My father will _____ home early today.

     A be
     B been
     C have been
     D has been

23. The man said he _____ going to call you later.

     A were
     B would
     C was
     D weren't

24. They _____ TV on rainy days.

     A watching
     B watch
     C were watching
     D was watching

GO ON TO NEXT PAGE

Name _____ Date _____

Part 8

Directions: For questions 25–27, choose the letter of the sentence that best combines the two underlined sentences. Record your answer on the answer sheet.

Sample: **That old building will be torn down.**

The building is in the middle of the street.

A That old building will be torn down in the middle of the street.

B Because that old building is in the middle of the street, it will be torn down.

C That old building in the middle of the street will be torn down.

D In the middle of the street that old building will be torn down

Answer: The correct answer is *C*.

---

25. **The baker decorated the cake with icing.**

    The icing was chocolate.

    A The chocolate cake was decorated by the baker.

    B The baker decorated the cake with chocolate icing.

    C The baker decorated the chocolate cake.

    D The baker's cake was decorated with chocolate icing.

26. **I like to spend time reading books.**

    My cousin prefers to watch television.

    A I like to spend time reading books although my cousin prefers to watch television.

    B I like to spend time reading books because my cousin prefers to watch television.

    C My cousin watches television and reads books.

    D My cousin and I read books and watch television.

27. **The audience was very quiet.**

    The acrobat performed his high wire act.

    A The audience was very quiet, so the acrobat performed his high wire act.

    B The audience was very quiet while the acrobat performed his high wire act.

    C The acrobat performed his high wire act because the audience was very quiet.

    D The acrobat performed his high wire act when the audience was very quiet.

STOP

Suggested Time Limit: 24 minutes   Your time: _____

Check your work if you have time. Wait for instructions from your teacher.

Name_____ Date _____

UNIT IV: STUDY SKILLS

Lesson 1: Using a table of contents and index
Part one

DIRECTIONS ▶ The Table of Contents below was taken from a social studies book about the United States. Darken the circle for the correct answer to each question. Choose *D. none of these* if the correct answer is not given.

💡 **STRATEGY TIPS**

1. Find the key word for the information you need.
2. Read straight across for information on the chapter.

Table of Contents		Page
Chapter One	Lands and Climate	7
Chapter Two	Natural Resources	28
Chapter Three	Agriculture	50
Chapter Four	Mining and Industry	71
Chapter Five	Manufacturing	89
Chapter Six	Fishing for Food	132
Chapter Seven	Businesses, Large and Small	164
Chapter Eight	Trade Here and Abroad	197

Sample:

On which page does Chapter Six begin?

Ⓐ page 71   Ⓒ page 132
Ⓑ page 89   Ⓓ none of these

ANSWER

The correct answer is *C. page 132.* When you read straight across from Chapter Six, you see it begins on page 132.

✏️ **NOW TRY THESE**

Use the Table of Contents to answer questions 1–3.

1. Which chapter begins on page 50?

    Ⓐ Chapter Three Ⓑ Chapter Four Ⓒ Chapter Six Ⓓ none of these

2. Which chapter would have information about coal mines?

    Ⓐ Chapter Five Ⓑ Chapter Three Ⓒ Chapter Four Ⓓ none of these

3. Where would you look to find information about the climate in California?

    Ⓐ Chapter Two Ⓑ Chapter One Ⓒ Chapter Eight Ⓓ none of these

GO ON TO NEXT PAGE

Name_____   Date _____

Lesson 1: Using a table of contents and index
Part two

DIRECTIONS ▶ The index below was taken from a math book. Look at the index carefully, then answer the questions by darkening the circle for the correct answer. If there is no correct answer, darken the circle for *D. none of these.*

Addition
    basic facts, 2-5
Difference
    10, 64, 65
    estimating, 64, 65
Division
    basic facts, 116–123
    game, 243
    of a two digit number, 228–231

Fractions
    and sets, 138
    subtraction of, 162–167
Magic square
    77
Number line
    154
Temperature
    189, 197

Sample:
    On what page will you play
    a division game?
    Ⓐ 77   Ⓒ 243
    Ⓑ 154   Ⓓ none of these

ANSWER

The correct answer is
C. page 243. The index
shows that a game is in the
division section of this book.

NOW TRY THESE

4. What subtopic is listed with the topic "Fractions"?
    Ⓐ comparing   Ⓒ basic facts
    Ⓑ and sets   Ⓓ none of these

5. Which pages would have practice with basic addition facts?
    Ⓐ 6–9   Ⓒ 1–2
    Ⓑ 10–12   Ⓓ none of these

6. On which page would you learn about a number line?
    Ⓐ 77   Ⓒ 64
    Ⓑ 154   Ⓓ none of these

7. What would you find on page 189?
    Ⓐ magic square   Ⓒ temperature
    Ⓑ estimating   Ⓓ none of these

STOP

Your time: _____   Number right: _____

On this lesson I did _____ because _____

_____.

Name_____   Date _____

Lesson 2: Using dictionary skills
Part one

DIRECTIONS ▶ Opposite each pair of guide words below are four words. For questions 1–3, darken the circle for the correct answer about the words.

 **STRATEGY TIPS**

1. Study each pair of dictionary guide words.
2. Use the rules of alphabetizing to determine which words would be on that dictionary page.

bottom	**bowl**	box, bound, bough, bout
even	**examine**	example, evil, easy, evade
oboe	**ocean**	obtain, occur, observe, oceanic
whirl	**who**	white, whip, whisk, whisper

Sample:
   Which word <u>would not</u> be between the guide words *bottom* and *bowl*?

   Ⓐ box   Ⓑ bound   Ⓒ bough   Ⓓ bout

 ANSWER

   The correct answer is *A. box. Box* would be on a page that comes after the word *bowl*.

 **NOW TRY THESE**

1. Which word <u>would</u> be between the guide words *even* and *examine*?

   Ⓐ example   Ⓑ easy   Ⓒ evil   Ⓓ evade

2. Which word <u>would not</u> be between the guide words *oboe* and *ocean*?

   Ⓐ obtain   Ⓑ occur   Ⓒ observe   Ⓓ oceanic

3. Which word <u>would not</u> be between *whirl* and *who*?

   Ⓐ white   Ⓑ whip   Ⓒ whisk   Ⓓ whisper

 GO ON TO NEXT PAGE

Name_____ Date _____

Lesson 2: Using dictionary skills
Part two

DIRECTIONS ▶ For questions 4–6, darken the circle of the number that best defines the underlined word as it is used in the sentence. Darken the circle for *D. none of these* if the correct answer is not given.

💡 **STRATEGY TIPS**

1   Try each dictionary definition in the sentence to find which one makes sense.
2. Read the sentence carefully looking for context clues about what the word means.

> **coach** *n.* 1. A large, four-wheeled, horse-drawn carriage. 2 A railroad passenger car. 3. A bus. 4. A teacher who trains students. 5. An instructor in athletics, debating, or dramatics.
>
> **coarse** *adj.* 1. Of poor quality or appearance; rough; common. 2. Made up of large particles; not fine; as, *coarse* sand. 3. Rude; vulgar.
>
> **smart** *v.* 1. To cause a stinging pain.—*adj.* 1. Quick to learn or do; clever. 2. Very active and alert. 3. Very stylish; fashionable.
>
> **vein** *n.* 1. One of the blood vessels that carry the blood back to the heart. 2. A streak of a different color or texture; as white marble with *veins* of gray. 3. A crack in rock filled with a mineral substance; as, a *vein* of gold.

Sample:

The pain in my arm began to smart.

Ⓐ adj. 2   Ⓒ v. 1
Ⓑ adj. 3   Ⓓ none of these

⚡ ANSWER

The correct answer is *C. v. 1*. The definition of smart in this sentence is to cause a stinging pain.

✏️ **NOW TRY THESE**

4. I needed to use coarse sandpaper for my woodworking project.

Ⓐ 1   Ⓑ 2   Ⓒ 3   Ⓓ none of these

5. Derek's tennis coach said that he was a good player.

Ⓐ 2   Ⓑ 3   Ⓒ 5   Ⓓ none of these

6. The prospector struck a vein of gold in the mountain.

Ⓐ 1   Ⓑ 2   Ⓒ 3   Ⓓ none of these

🛑 **STOP**

Your time: _____   Number right: _____

On this lesson I did _____ because _____ .

Name_____   Date _____

Lesson 3: Using map skills
Part one

 **DIRECTIONS** ▶ Darken the circle for the correct answer.

💡 **STRATEGY TIPS**

1. The compass rose will help you find north, south, east, and west.
2. Use a ruler to measure distance between two places and multiply inches by miles given on the mileage key.

Sample:

Which of the following symbols on a map would mean railroad tracks?

Ⓐ    Ⓒ

Ⓑ    Ⓓ ┼┼┼┼┼┼

⚡ **ANSWER**

The correct answer is
D ┼┼┼┼┼┼ . This symbol tells you that there are railroad tracks.

✏️ **NOW TRY THESE**

1. If you want to know what the symbols on a map stand for, look at the _____ .

   Ⓐ map key   Ⓒ compass rose
   Ⓑ scale drawing Ⓓ map directions

2. The imaginary line going from east to west that is used to divide Earth into two equal parts is called _____ .

   Ⓐ latitude   Ⓒ equator
   Ⓑ longitude   Ⓓ Prime Meridian

3. Which kind of map would be most helpful when you go on a car trip to another state?

   Ⓐ relief map   Ⓒ street map
   Ⓑ road map   Ⓓ aerial map

4. From the compass rose pictured here, you can tell that east is

   _____ .

   Ⓐ to the left of north
   Ⓑ opposite north
   Ⓒ to the right of north
   Ⓓ opposite south

5. Which of the following symbols on a map would mean mountains?

   Ⓐ 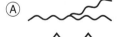   Ⓒ

   Ⓑ    Ⓓ

6. What do the the letters SW on a compass rose mean?

   Ⓐ southwest   Ⓒ northeast
   Ⓑ southeast   Ⓓ northwest

GO ON TO NEXT PAGE

Name_____   Date _____

Lesson 3: Using map skills
Part two

DIRECTIONS ▶ Darken the circle for the correct answer found on the map.

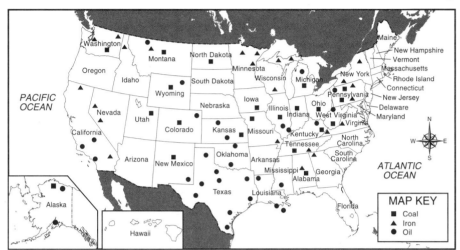

Sample:

Which state has no coal, iron, or oil?

Ⓐ New Mexico   Ⓒ North Dakota
Ⓑ Texas   Ⓓ Arizona

ANSWER

The correct answer is *D. Arizona.*

NOW TRY THESE

7. Which state has the most oil?

   Ⓐ Tennessee   Ⓒ Texas
   Ⓑ California   Ⓓ Alabama

8. Which two states have only coal and iron?

   Ⓐ California, Illinois
   Ⓑ Tennessee, Alabama
   Ⓒ Kansas, Colorado
   Ⓓ Alabama, California

9. Name the state that has only iron and oil.

   Ⓐ California   Ⓒ Pennsylvania
   Ⓑ Maine   Ⓓ Wyoming

10. What three states have coal, iron, and oil?

    Ⓐ Pennsylvania, Texas, California
    Ⓑ Illinois, Minnesota, Louisiana
    Ⓒ Michigan, Illinois, Pennsylvania
    Ⓓ Pennsylvania, Montana, Michigan

STOP

Your time: _____   Number right: _____

On this lesson I did _____ because _____

_____ .

Name_____ Date _____

Lesson 4: Reading charts, diagrams, and graphs
Part one

DIRECTIONS ▶ Study the graph below. Then for questions 1–3, darken the circle for the correct answer. Darken the circle for *D. not given* if the information is not on the graph.

💡 **STRATEGY TIPS**

1. The numbers on the left of the graph tell how many.
2. The names on the bottom of the graph tell what.

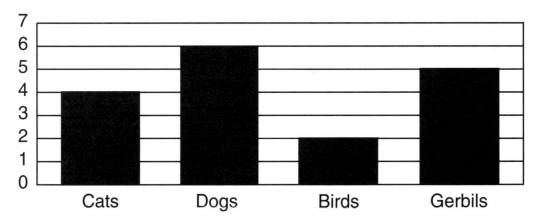

Sample:

How many children live on Garrett's street?

Ⓐ 6   Ⓒ 12
Ⓑ 3   Ⓓ not given

ANSWER

The correct answer is *D. not given*. This chart does not show the number of children on the street.

✏️ **NOW TRY THESE**

1. Which is the largest number of animals shown on the graph?

   Ⓐ dogs   Ⓑ gerbils   Ⓒ cats   Ⓓ birds

2. From this graph you can tell that there are twice as many cats as

   _____ .

   Ⓐ gerbils   Ⓑ dogs   Ⓒ birds   Ⓓ not given

3. What is the total number of pets shown on the graph?

   Ⓐ 17   Ⓑ 10   Ⓒ 12   Ⓓ not given

Name_____ Date _____

Lesson 4: Reading charts, diagrams, and graphs

Part two

DIRECTIONS ▶ For questions 4–6, study the chart below carefully. Then darken the circle for the correct answer. Darken the circle for *D. not given* if the information is not on the chart.

STRATEGY TIPS

1. Find the information from the question on the chart.
2. Then look at the other information on the same line to answer the question.

GOLF CLUBS, DISTANCES, AND USES		
Club	*Distance*	*Use*
Woods		
1	150–180 yards	Drive from the tee
2	140–170 yards	Drive from fairway with good lie
3	130–150 yards	On fairway for lift and distance
4	120–140 yards	On fairway for lift and distance
Irons		
5	100–130 yards	On fairway for lift and distance and in the rough
7	80–110 yards	Approach to green
Putter		On the green

Sample:

Which iron could you use as you approach the green at 100 yards?

Ⓐ 4 wood   Ⓒ 7 iron
Ⓑ putter   Ⓓ not given

ANSWER

The correct answer is *C. 7 iron*. When you find "approach to green" and "100 yards" on the chart, you find the 7 iron on the same line.

NOW TRY THESE

4. Which club would you use when you are on the green?

   Ⓐ 7 iron   Ⓑ putter   Ⓒ 4 wood   Ⓓ not given

5. Which club would you use to drive off the tee?

   Ⓐ 7 iron   Ⓑ 5 iron   Ⓒ 1 wood   Ⓓ not given

6. Which wood could you use on the fairway for a distance of 120 yards?

   Ⓐ 1 wood   Ⓑ 4 wood   Ⓒ 3 wood   Ⓓ not given

GO ON TO NEXT PAGE

Name_____   Date _____

Lesson 4: Reading charts, diagrams, and graphs
Part three

DIRECTIONS ▶ For questions 7–10, study the picture graph carefully. Then darken the circle for the correct answer to the questions. Darken the circle for *D. not given* if the information is not on the graph.

STRATEGY TIPS

1. The left part of the graph tells you which city.
2. The key tells you that each symbol stands for a given number.

Number of Sunny Days in Some U.S. Cities in 1995

Miami, FL

Austin, TX

San Francisco, CA

Cleveland, OH

New York, NY

KEY: Each ☼ stands for 20 days.

NOW TRY THESE

7. How many sunny days does one symbol stand for?

   Ⓐ 20 days   Ⓒ 30 days
   Ⓑ 10 days   Ⓓ 1 day

8. Which city had the least number of sunny days?

   Ⓐ Austin   Ⓒ Cleveland
   Ⓑ San Francisco Ⓓ Miami

9. Which city had almost as many sunny days as Austin?

   Ⓐ Miami   Ⓒ New York
   Ⓑ San Francisco Ⓓ Cleveland

10. Which city had more than 200 sunny days?

    Ⓐ Austin   Ⓒ New York
    Ⓑ Cleveland Ⓓ San Francisco

STOP

Your time: _____

Number right: _____

On this lesson I did _____ because _____

_____.

Name_____   Date _____

PRACTICE TEST 4

Part 1

Directions: For questions 1–3, use the Table of Contents. Record your answer on the answer sheet.

Table of Contents

Sample: **This book is about _____ .**

A pets
B living on a farm
C different kinds of animals
D zoo animals

Answer: The correct answer is *C. different kinds of animals.*

---

1. **Which chapter would have information about elephants?**

   A Chapter 5
   B Chapter 3
   C Chapter 2
   D Chapter 4

2. **Where would you look to find out how to care for a pet?**

   A Chapter 1
   B Chapter 3
   C Chapter 5
   D Chapter 2

3. **Which chapter would probably have information about turtles?**

   A Chapter 2
   B Chapter 4
   C Chapter 3
   D Chapter 1

Name _____   Date _____

Part 2

Directions: For questions 4–6, record your answer on the answer sheet. Use the index.

Regrouping
      addition with, 28–29
      more than once, 42–43
      subtraction with, 40–41
    Remainders, 88–89
    Rounding, 12–13
      decimals, 324–325
      in estimating costs, 356–357

Sample: **What topic would you find on page 12?**

    A addition with
    B rounding
    C estimating
    D decimals

Answer: The correct answer is *B. rounding.*

---

4. **Which subtopic is listed under the topic "Regrouping"?**

    A subtraction with
    B remainders
    C rounding
    D decimals

5. **Which pages would have practice on addition with regrouping?**

    A 42–43
    B 12–13
    C 28–29
    D 88–89

6. **On which page would you first read about rounding?**

    A 324
    B 356
    C 88
    D 12

Name_____ Date _____

Part 3

Directions: For questions 7–9, use the guide words. Record your answer on the answer sheet.

Guide Words
dresser–drone
halibut–hand
mold–monk
ranger–ratio

Sample: Which word <u>would not</u> be between the guide words *mold* and *monk*?

    A money
    B molt
    C moment
    D molar

Answer: The correct answer is *D. molar.*

---

7. Which word <u>would</u> be between the <u>guide words</u> *dresser* and *drone*?

    A dress
    B driver
    C drool
    D dream

8. Which word <u>would</u> be between the <u>guide words</u> *mold* and *monk*?

    A monkey
    B month
    C mongrel
    D moist

9. Which word <u>would not</u> be between the <u>guide words</u> *ranger* and *ratio*?

    A rate
    B rang
    C rash
    D rare

GO ON TO NEXT PAGE

Name_____   Date _____

Part 4

Directions: For questions 10–12, choose the number that best defines the underlined word as it is used in the sentence. Choose *D. none of these* if the answer is not given. Record your answer on the answer sheet.

> **blue** *adj.* 1. Of the color blue. 2. Low in spirits; sad; discouraged. 3. *n.* The color in the rainbow between green and violet.
>
> **blow** *v.* 1. To send forth a strong current of air. 2. To make a sound by blowing, as on a whistle. 3. To destroy by explosion.
>
> **crank** *n.* 1. In a machine, a part or arm which can be turned to start machinery. 2. An irritable person. 3. *v.* To operate by turning a crank.

Sample:

She could not find her blue crayon.

  A 3   **B** 2   **C** 1   **D** none of these

Answer: The correct answer is *C. 1.* In this sentence, *blue* means *of the color blue.*

---

10. **I always feel blue on a rainy day.**

  A 1   **B** 2   **C** 3   **D** none of these

11. **They planned to blow up all of the balloons.**

  A 1   **B** 2   **C** 3   **D** none of these

12. **Turn the crank in order to start the engine.**

  A 1   **B** 2   **C** 3   **D** none of these

GO ON TO NEXT PAGE

Name_____   Date _____

Part 5

Directions: For questions 13–18, record your answer on the answer sheet. Use the map.

Sample: Near what body of water is the ballfield?

   A Pacific Ocean
   B San Francisco Bay
   C Atlantic Ocean
   D Mississippi River

Answer:
The correct answer is
B. San Francisco Bay.

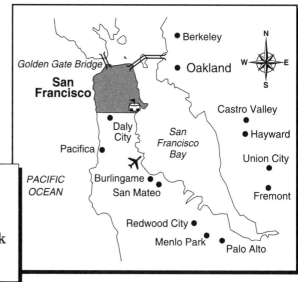

Key

✈ Airport
🏟 Ball Park
═ Bridge

---

13. What ocean lies west of San Francisco?

   A Atlantic Ocean
   B San Francisco Bay
   C Pacific Ocean
   D San Francisco Ocean

14. The airport is nearest to what city?

   A San Mateo
   B Burlingame
   C Pacifica
   D Daly City

15. Menlo Park lies between what two cities?

   A Palo Alto, Redwood City
   B Fremont, Burlingame
   C San Mateo, Redwood City
   D Pacifica, Hayward

16. If you traveled directly west of Fremont, what city would you reach?

   A Redwood City
   B San Mateo
   C Berkeley
   D Pacifica

17. In which directions does the Golden Gate Bridge take drivers?

   A north, south
   B east, west
   C north, east
   D south, west

18. In which direction would you need to drive from Oakland to reach Pacifica?

   A southwest
   B northeast
   C southeast
   D northwest

Name_____   Date _____

Part 6

Directions: For questions 19–21, record your answer on the answer sheet. Use the picture graph.

Number of Books on Each Shelf in the Bookcase

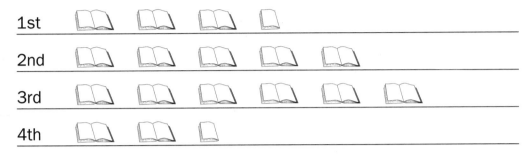

KEY: Each [book] **stands for 10 books**

Sample: **Which shelf has the most books?**

    A 1st
    B 2nd
    C 3rd
    D 4th

Answer: The correct answer is *C. 3rd.*

---

19. Which shelf has fewer than 35 books?

    A 1st
    B 2nd
    C 3rd
    D 4th

20. How many books are there altogether?

    A 85
    B 60
    C 170
    D 145

21. How many books does each symbol represent?

    A 20
    B 15
    C 5
    D 10

GO ON TO NEXT PAGE

Name_____   Date _____

Part 7

Directions: For questions 22–24, record your answer on the answer sheet.

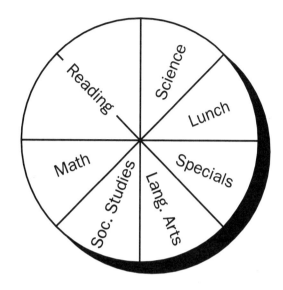

22. **How many periods are there in the school day?**

    A 6
    B 8
    C 7
    D 9

23. **How many periods are used for reading class?**

    A 3
    B 1
    C 2
    D 4

24. **Reading clockwise, which period comes after lunch?**

    A math
    B science
    C specials
    D language arts

STOP

Suggested Time Limit: 20 minutes   Your time: _____
Check your work if you have time. Wait for instructions from your teacher.

Name_____ Date _____

UNIT V: READING COMPREHENSION

Lesson 1: Recognizing main ideas

DIRECTIONS ▶ Darken the circle for the title that tells the main idea of each paragraph.

 **STRATEGY TIPS**

1. Think about the whole paragraph.
2. What is the author trying to tell you?

Sample:

Some high school students have after-school jobs. Many states allow students to get working papers after they turn 14. There are rules about the kind of work students can do. They cannot work at dangerous jobs. There are rules about the number of hours and the times of day students can work.

A good title for this paragraph is:

Ⓐ Why Students Work After School
Ⓑ Getting a Good Job
Ⓒ Rules for Working After School
Ⓓ How to Get Working Papers

ANSWER

The correct answer is *C. Rules for Working After School.* The author is trying to tell you about rules for students.

NOW TRY THESE

1. Several years ago a horse named Charon won six races. He earned $93,000. Charon won the races because he is afraid of other horses. When Charon sees horses near him, he tries to get away from them. He gets away by running fast and staying out in front, often winning the race.

A good title for this paragraph would be:

Ⓐ Winning Six Races
Ⓑ Why Charon Wins Races
Ⓒ Dean Watson's Horse
Ⓓ How to Win $93,000

2. Opossums are amazing little animals. When a hunter finds an opossum, it may be putting on an act of being "dead." It's "playing possum." A person can tweak the opossum's whiskers or pull on its toes and there is no sign of life. The opossum doesn't seem to be breathing and it's hard to find a heartbeat.

A good title for this paragraph is:

Ⓐ Hunting For Opossum
Ⓑ Playing Possum
Ⓒ How A Possum Breathes
Ⓓ Many Amazing Little Animals

GO ON TO NEXT PAGE

Test Taking 4, SV 6773-5

Name_____ Date _____

Unit 5, lesson 1, page 2

3. Some authors don't use their real names when they write books. They use a pen name. Mark Twain's real name was Samuel Clemens. When he was a young man he used to guide boats on the Mississippi River. When the water is two fathoms deep, it is called "mark twain." Samuel Clemens signed all his books, including Tom Sawyer, with his pen name.

A good title for this book is:

Ⓐ Guiding Boats on the Mississippi
Ⓑ Samuel Clemens's Pen Name
Ⓒ How to Choose a Pen Name
Ⓓ Tom Sawyer's Real Name

4. Moe Berg was a scholar and an athlete. He had a degree from Princeton University. He could speak and write in 12 languages. For a living, Berg played major league baseball. In 1928, he led American League catchers in the least number of errors. He was nominated for the Most Valuable Player.

A good title for this paragraph is:

Ⓐ A Scholarly Ballplayer
Ⓑ Most Valuable Player
Ⓒ A Greek Ballplayer
Ⓓ Reading Newspapers In Twelve Languages

STOP

Your time: _____

Number right: _____

On this lesson I did _____ because _____

_____ .

I think it would help me to _____

_____

_____ .

Name_____   Date _____

Lesson 2: Finding sentences that do not belong

DIRECTIONS ▶ Darken the circle for the sentence that <u>does not</u> belong in each paragraph.

💡 **STRATEGY TIPS**

1. Read the entire paragraph.
2. Think about the main idea of the paragraph.
3. Decide which sentence <u>does not</u> support the main idea.

Sample:

(1) You can read a newspaper in any order. (2) There are many different kinds of newspapers in the United States. (3) Some people start by reading the headlines on the front page. (4) Others go straight to the sports, comics, or television page.

Ⓐ Sentence 1   Ⓒ Sentence 3
Ⓑ Sentence 2   Ⓓ Sentence 4

ANSWER

The correct answer is *B. Sentence 2*. This sentence is not about the order a newspaper is read.

NOW TRY THESE

1. (1) About one out of ten people is left-handed. (2) Long ago people thought that lefties were witches or crooks. (3) Some people can use either hand equally well. (4) Now scientists have proven that left-handers may be more creative than right-handers.

Ⓐ Sentence 1   Ⓒ Sentence 3
Ⓑ Sentence 2   Ⓓ Sentence 4

2. (1) Terns are fish-eating birds. (2) The Arctic tern migrates from one end of Earth to the other. (3) It flies from the Arctic to the Antarctic and back each year. (4) The round trip is about 23,000 miles.

Ⓐ Sentence 1   Ⓒ Sentence 3
Ⓑ Sentence 2   Ⓓ Sentence 4

GO ON TO NEXT PAGE

Name_____   Date _____

Unit 5, lesson 2, page 2

3. (1) Willie Shoemaker was a successful American jockey. (2) During his career he rode 8,514 winners. (3) In one year he won 485 races. (4) Many people enjoy going to the racetrack.

Ⓐ Sentence 1   Ⓒ Sentence 3
Ⓑ Sentence 2   Ⓓ Sentence 4

4. (1) Wolfgang Mozart was a musical genius. (2) He started playing musical instruments when he was three and wrote two minuets when he was five years old. (3) Mozart always wore very fashionable clothes. (4) By the age of fourteen, his first opera was performed.

Ⓐ Sentence 1   Ⓒ Sentence 3
Ⓑ Sentence 2   Ⓓ Sentence 4

5. (1) Many animals have tails. (2) They use their tails for many different purposes. (3) Horses and cows can flick their tails back and forth to get rid of flies and bugs. (4) A manx is a kind of cat that doesn't have a tail.

Ⓐ Sentence 1   Ⓒ Sentence 3
Ⓑ Sentence 2   Ⓓ Sentence 4

STOP

Your time: _____

Number right: _____

On this lesson I did _____ because _____

_____ .

I think it would help me to _____

_____

_____ .

Name_____   Date _____

Lesson 3: Arranging sentences in correct order

Part one

DIRECTIONS ▶ Darken the circle for the sentence that should come <u>first</u> in the following groups of sentences.

STRATEGY TIPS

1. When you read the sentences, look for signal words such as *first*, *next*, *later*, *so*, and *then*.
2. Signal words help you decide the correct order for the sentences.

Sample:

Ⓐ Then, she climbed into the canoe.
Ⓑ Erin always puts on her life jacket before she goes canoeing.
Ⓒ Next, she untied it from the dock and got her paddle in hand.
Ⓓ Finally, she headed out onto the lake.

ANSWER

The correct answer is *B. Erin always puts on her life jacket before she goes canoeing*. The signal word is *before*. The other sentences tell what she did after putting on her life jacket.

NOW TRY THESE

1. Ⓐ Next, whisk in milk and pepper.
   Ⓑ Cook the egg mixture in a frying pan, stirring constantly.
   Ⓒ To make scrambled eggs, you must first break two eggs into a bowl.
   Ⓓ Finally, enjoy the scrambled eggs with toast.

2. Ⓐ It's possible that millions of years ago, a huge meteorite hit Earth and caused dinosaurs to become extinct.
   Ⓑ Since plant-eating dinosaurs had no food, they all died.
   Ⓒ With no sunlight, all the plants died.
   Ⓓ After the meteorite hit, it caused a huge cloud of dust to shut out sunlight.

GO ON TO NEXT PAGE

Name_____ Date _____

Unit 5, lesson 3, page 2

3. Ⓐ Chop all of the vegetables into bite-sized pieces.
   Ⓑ Next, heat oil in a wok.
   Ⓒ Then add the vegetables, stirring the whole time, to make a delicious meal.
   Ⓓ Before making a stir fry meal, always wash your hands and each of the vegetables thoroughly.

4. Ⓐ Tie a napkin around your neck and dig in!
   Ⓑ Cover it with whipped cream and a cherry on top.
   Ⓒ Next, pour syrup over the top of the ice cream.
   Ⓓ To make a sundae, put two scoops of vanilla ice cream in a bowl.

5. Ⓐ Soon pellets of rain began to fall.
   Ⓑ Hail, lightning, and strong winds soon followed.
   Ⓒ At first I noticed the dark clouds on the horizon.
   Ⓓ When the storm was over, I was relieved there had been no damage.

6. Ⓐ The Siberian tiger spends much of its time hunting.
   Ⓑ The tiger drags the prey to cover, eats its fill, and covers the remains to eat later after resting.
   Ⓒ Then the tiger pounces and grabs the prey by the back of the neck, killing it.
   Ⓓ First, it creeps to within 30 to 80 feet of its prey.

—————————————————————————————————————— **STOP**

Your time: _____

Number right: _____

On this lesson I did _____ because _____

_____ .

I think it would help me to _____

_____ .

Name_____   Date _____

Lesson 3: Arranging sentences in correct order

Part two

DIRECTIONS ▶ Darken the circle of the sentence which should come <u>last</u> in each of the following groups of sentences.

STRATEGY TIPS

1. Think about the correct order of the events.
2. Then find the sentence that should end the paragraph.

Sample:

Ⓐ It swims across the water using its front legs, with hind legs trailing behind.

Ⓑ The polar bear dives off the iceberg into the water.

Ⓒ When it climbs back onto the ice, it shakes the water from its coat before it freezes.

Ⓓ Then the bear closes its nostrils and dives under the water.

ANSWER

The correct answer is *C. When it climbs back onto the ice, it shakes the water from its coat before it freezes.* The *last* thing the bear does is climb back onto the ice.

NOW TRY THESE

7. Ⓐ The cubs remain with their mother into the third spring of their lives.

Ⓑ In October and November, polar bears dig dens for giving birth.

Ⓒ Bear cubs are born hairless, blind, and deaf in November or December.

Ⓓ The mother and her cubs stay in the den until March or April.

8. Ⓐ The birds that live in the southern United States begin their return migration in February.

Ⓑ They return to the U.S. in time for the flowering of their food plants.

Ⓒ In the fall, the ruby-throated hummingbird begins its migration south.

Ⓓ The birds migrate more than 1,850 miles from the eastern United States to winter in Central America.

GO ON TO NEXT PAGE

Name_____   Date _____

Unit 5, lesson 3, part 2, page 2

9. Ⓐ All day the octopus stays hidden in its nest.
   Ⓑ The octopus digs a gravel nest.
   Ⓒ Then, at night, it comes out to hunt, changing color to blend in with its surroundings.
   Ⓓ The octopus hunts by grabbing a crab, crayfish, or mollusk with its long arms, using suckers to grip its slippery prey.

10. Ⓐ The first sign of spring is often buds on a tree.
    Ⓑ Soon, green leaves emerge.
    Ⓒ Day by day, the buds open into flowers.
    Ⓓ When summer arrives, the tree is covered in leaves.

11. Ⓐ The audience jumps to its feet and applauds the beautiful performance.
    Ⓑ The music begins quietly, growing louder.
    Ⓒ Dancers leap across the stage.
    Ⓓ As the music ends, the dancers slowly leave the stage.

12. Ⓐ She drops pasta into the boiling water.
    Ⓑ First, the chef puts water on to boil.
    Ⓒ Finally, she tops the pasta with tomato sauce and grated cheese.
    Ⓓ Next, she pours the pasta into a strainer to drain off the water.

STOP

Your time: _____

Number right: _____

On this lesson I did _____ because _____

_____ .

I think it would help me to _____

_____ .

Name_____   Date _____

Lesson 4: Reading stories

 **DIRECTIONS** ▶ Darken the circle for the correct answer to each question about the story.

💡 **STRATEGY TIPS**

1 Look at the questions before you read the story.
2. Read the story, then read the questions again.
3 Check your answers by looking back at the story.

Sample: The most dangerous part of a space flight comes at the end. When a spaceship returns from a mission, it moves very fast. As it enters Earth's atmosphere, the spaceship gets extremely hot. The heat shield on the ship keeps it cool and protects the astronauts. The heat shield must be facing up when the spaceship enters the atmosphere. Otherwise, the ship would burn up.

The purpose of the heat shield is to:

ⓐ Keep the spaceship moving fast.
ⓑ Enter the Earth's atmosphere.
ⓒ Always face up during a space flight.
ⓓ Keep the spaceship cool when it enters the atmosphere.

ANSWER

The correct answer is *D. Keep the spaceship cool when it enters the atmosphere.* The fourth sentence in this paragraph tells you that the heat shield keeps the spaceship cool when it is returning to Earth.

GO ON TO NEXT PAGE

Name_____   Date _____

Unit 5, lesson 4, page 2

NOW TRY THESE

Passage 1

Although Margaret Gaffney Haughery never learned to read or write, she became a successful business woman.

When Margaret was five years old, she came to America with her parents. Four years later, Margaret's parents died and she was raised by neighbors.

As an adult, Margaret worked in a laundry and spent her free time working with children at a local orphanage. She saved enough money to buy some cows and open her own dairy business. Her business was successful, and she was able to build a home for orphans.

Margaret eventually sold her dairy and opened a bakery. Her bakery was the first in the South to be run by steam. It produced and sold crackers and soon became New Orleans' largest export business, selling crackers to other countries. Margaret earned the nickname, "the bread woman of New Orleans."

Margaret Gaffney Haughery never stopped helping people in need. During her life, she helped build ten homes for children and elderly people.

1. Margaret was _____ years old when her parents died.
   - (A) 5
   - (B) 4
   - (C) 9
   - (D) 18

2. Where did Margaret spend her free time when she worked at a laundry?
   - (A) at a bakery
   - (B) at a laundry
   - (C) at a dairy farm
   - (D) at an orphanage

3. When you export something, you _____ .
   - (A) package it
   - (B) send it to another country
   - (C) help people in need
   - (D) build homes for elderly people

4. Although she never learned to read or write, you could say that Margaret was _____ .
   - (A) sad
   - (B) smart
   - (C) angry
   - (D) foolish

GO ON TO NEXT PAGE

Name_____   Date _____

Unit 5, lesson 4, page 3

Passage II

Wee Willie Keeler of Baltimore set a major league baseball record in 1897—making a hit in 44 straight games! During the summer of 1941, New York Yankee Joe Di Maggio surpassed 44 games and broke Keeler's record.

Newspapers reported about Joe's hitting streak every day. How long could his streak last? When would it end? Joe was modest about his talent. He never bragged or boasted.

By the night of July 17, 1941, Joe had had a hit in 55 straight games. During his fifty-sixth game, he was tagged out at first his first two times at bat. Then, in the eighth inning, Joe hit the ball. But he was out in a double play. Joe would not get another chance to bat in that game.

Joe's teammates thought he'd be upset. Even though the Yankees won the game, Joe's historic hitting streak was over. Joe walked into the locker room and said, "Well, that's over."

The newspapers called him, "Joltin' Joe Di Maggio." A popular song was written about his hitting streak. Yet through it all, Joe remained modest and unassuming.

5. For what team did Joe Di Maggio play?

Ⓐ Baltimore Orioles
Ⓑ New York Yankees
Ⓒ Boston Braves
Ⓓ Montreal Expos

6. What happened when Joe hit into a double play?

Ⓐ His teammates were nervous.
Ⓑ Everyone wondered how long his streak would last.
Ⓒ Joe was upset.
Ⓓ Joe's hitting streak was over.

7. The author says Joe was modest because _____ .

Ⓐ he bragged about his hitting streak
Ⓑ he didn't get along with his teammates
Ⓒ he was quiet and unassuming
Ⓓ everyone was talking about him

8. Joe's hitting streak was historic because _____ .

Ⓐ the Yankees won the game
Ⓑ he was the first player to break Wee Willie Keeler's record
Ⓒ Wee Willie Keelers's streak happened in 1897
Ⓓ they wrote a song about it

Name_____   Date _____

Unit 5, lesson 4, page 4

Passage III

Nowhere else on Earth is there a symbol that stands for the ideals of freedom as dramatically as the Statue of Liberty.

The statue, a gift from the people of France to the people of the United States, was placed on Bedloe's Island in New York Harbor in 1886. It was designed by a Frenchman named Frederic-Auguste Bartholdi. The pedestal was designed by an American named Richard Morris Hunt.

The statue was unveiled on October 28, 1886. Unveiling day was a public holiday. On that rainy and foggy day in October, more than a million people lined the streets to watch a special parade in honor of the statue.

Today Bedloe's Island is called Liberty Island. Each year thousands of visitors take a boat to Liberty Island to see this famous symbol.

9. Another word for symbol could be
   _____ .

   Ⓐ image
   Ⓑ flag
   Ⓒ holiday
   Ⓓ gift

10. From the story you can tell that
    _____.

    Ⓐ French people and American people didn't get along
    Ⓑ Richard Hunt didn't like the statue
    Ⓒ nobody cared about the statue
    Ⓓ the statue means a lot to many people

11. When a work of art is unveiled, it is
    _____ .

    Ⓐ draped in fabric
    Ⓑ uncovered
    Ⓒ polished
    Ⓓ covered over

12. According to this story, the Statue of Liberty is _____ .

    Ⓐ almost 100 years old
    Ⓑ not very large
    Ⓒ more than 100 years old
    Ⓓ thousands of years old

STOP

Your time: _____

Number right: _____

On this lesson I did _____ because _____

_____ .

I think it would help me to _____ .

Name_____   Date _____

PRACTICE TEST 5

Part 1

Directions: For questions 1–3, choose the title that tells the main idea of each paragraph. Record your answer on the answer sheet.

Sample: On September 16, 1620, a group of 100 men, women, and children left England on a ship called the Mayflower. The trip would take them across the Atlantic Ocean to make new homes in Virginia. Their three-month journey was difficult. They finally reached dry land at Plymouth Rock, Massachusetts, on December 26. The weary travelers decided against going on to Virginia, and settled in Massachusetts.

    A A Ship Called the Mayflower
    B People of Plymouth Rock
    C New Homes In Virginia
    D A Long and Difficult Journey

Answer: The correct answer is *D. A Long and Difficult Journey.*

---

1. A small lizard, called a gecko, has a special way of protecting itself. When attacked it simply drops off its tail. The tail keeps wriggling on the ground, confusing attackers. Soon new cells will grow where the tail dropped off. This growth is called a bud. After about eight to twelve months, the gecko has a new, full-sized tail.

    A A Wriggling Tail   **C** Growing A New Tail
    B How Geckos Protect Themselves   **D** From Cells to Buds

2. Ants are called social insects because they live and work together. Some of their nests have less than fifty ants and some have thousands of ants. Their nests can be found under stones, in hollow stems, under the bark of trees, and in the ground. We most often see the kind of ants that have nests on the ground. Usually their nests have more than one opening. The openings are sometimes hidden.

    A Social Insects   **C** Finding Ant Nests
    B Thousands of Ants   **D** Ants and Their Nests

GO ON TO NEXT PAGE

Name_____   Date _____

3. When the Revolutionary War began, the American colonies stopped using the English flag. Each one of the thirteen colonies used a different flag. This was so confusing that George Washington wrote to Congress and said, "Please fix some flag by which our vessels will know each other."

A Why the Colonies Needed One Flag
B Flags of the Thirteen Colonies
C How We Won the Revolutionary War
D Using the English Flag

Part 2

Directions: For questions 4–5, choose the sentence that <u>does not</u> belong in each paragraph. Record your answer on the answer sheet.

Sample: (1) General Washington discussed a design for a flag with Robert Morris and Colonel George Ross. (2) The men were all good friends. (3) They consulted with Colonel Ross's niece, Mistress Betsy Ross. (4) Mistress Ross helped them decide on a design for the first American flag.

A Sentence 1	**C** Sentence 3
B Sentence 2	**D** Sentence 4

Answer: The correct answer is *B. Sentence 2.*

4. (1) People like to look at statues of animals. (2) A statue of Balto, the dog, stands in Central Park, New York. (3) Balto was a sled dog who was part of the United States Postal Service in Alaska. (4) In the winter of 1925, he carried a life-saving serum more than "600 miles over rough ice, across treacherous waters, through Arctic blizzards" to save the children of Nome, Alaska.

A Sentence 1   **C** Sentence 3
B Sentence 2   **D** Sentence 4

5. (1) Bird-watching is a hobby enjoyed by many people. (2) Birds can fly great distances. (3) Birds are identified by their color, flight, and song. (4) Bird-watchers often use books to help them identify the birds they see.

A Sentence 1   **C** Sentence 3
B Sentence 2   **D** Sentence 4

GO ON TO NEXT PAGE

Name_____   Date _____

Part 3

Directions: For question 6, choose the letter for the sentence which should come <u>first</u> in the paragraph. Record your answer on the answer sheet.

Sample: **A** Soon all the children were buckled in.
B Finally, the Jacksons arrived at their grandparents' house.
C Before leaving on vacation, Mr. Jackson put the luggage in the trunk of the car.
D They sang songs as the car traveled along the highway.

Answer: The correct answer is *C. Before leaving on vacation, Mr. Jackson put the luggage in the trunk of the car.* This sentence tells what they did *before* leaving.

---

6. **A** Then the plane taxied down the runway.
B The flight attendant closed the jet door.
C Next, she made sure all the passengers were wearing seat belts.
D Finally, they were in the air!

Part 4

Directions: For question 7, choose the letter for the sentence which should come <u>last</u> in the paragraph. Record your answer on the answer sheet.

Sample: **A** Rachel rowed the boat out to the middle of the lake.
B Then she waited and waited for a fish to bite.
C They weren't biting, so Rachel rowed back to the dock.
D She hooked the bait onto the fishing line.

Answer: The correct answer is *C. They weren't biting, so Rachel rowed back to the dock.* This sentence best completes the paragraph.

---

7. **A** I always leave with an armload.
B Then I sit and look at magazines and newspapers.
C I look at books on every imaginable subject.
D I like to spend the day at the public library.

Name_____   Date _____

Part 5

Directions: For questions 8–18, choose the correct answer to each question about the story. Record your answer on the answer sheet.

Sample: Many tourists visit Mount Rushmore in the Black Hills of South Dakota. They go to see the sixty-foot-tall carvings of the faces of four U.S. presidents.

Gutzon Borglum started the project in 1927. But he died in 1941 shortly before the work was completed. His son, Lincoln, finished his father's job. On Mount Rushmore the faces of George Washington, Thomas Jefferson, Theodore Roosevelt, and Abraham Lincoln can be seen sixty miles away.

Tourists visit Mount Rushmore because _____ .

A they enjoy mountain climbing
B Lincoln Borglum helped his father
C there are many things to see
D they want to see the carvings of the presidents

Answer: The correct answer is *D. they want to see the carvings of the presidents.*

Passage I

"Aladdin" and "Sinbad's Voyages" are two of the wonderful stories found in the *Arabian Nights*. When were these stories told? Who first told them? Nobody knows for sure.

Long ago, a famous caliph, or emperor, named Harun-al-Rashid, ruled over a large part of Asia. Poets and storytellers in his palace told many stories for the caliph's entertainment. Stories were added to the collection until it grew to be the largest collection of stories in ancient Asia.

Little by little, these Eastern tales were translated into many languages. Today they are still read and enjoyed by people all over the world.

8. You can tell that the author thinks these stories are

_____ .

A collectible   **C** very good
B poetic   **D** old-fashioned

9. Caliph is another word for

_____ .

A entertainment   **C** Arabian
B languages   **D** emperor

10. We can read these stories today because _____ .

A they have been translated into English
B poets and storytellers told them
C they have been added to the collection
D they are wonderful

GO ON TO NEXT PAGE

Name_____   Date _____

Passage II

Hundreds of years ago, when Richard the Lion-Hearted was king, England was very different than it is today. There were no large cities and not many people. The island was almost completely covered with forests. Here and there in open spaces were cottages, farms, churches, and castles.

In one of these forests lived Robin Hood. We know very little about who he was or why he made his home in the forest. Some tales say he was the only son of the Earl of Huntingdon. These tales say that an enemy killed the earl and burned his castle, but Robin Hood escaped to Sherwood Forest.

Other tales say Robin Hood hid in the forest because he had shot one of the king's deer. In those days it was against the law to hunt or even walk in the king's forest, and a man could be put to death for breaking the law.

The stories differ as to why Robin went to the forest to live, but all the stories agree that he was a tall, strong, handsome man. They said that he was brave and fearless, the best archer in the land, generous and kind to women, children, and poor folk.

11. In the time of King Richard, England had _____ .

A many cities
B many forests
C many churches
D many castles

12. The author says that everyone _____ .

A knew why Robin lived in the forest
B liked to hunt deer
C walked in the king's forest
D thought that Robin was a brave and fearless man

13. An archer is someone who is skilled at _____ .

A using a bow and arrow
B living in a forest
C telling stories
D killing deer

14. One reason Robin might have lived in the forest is that he _____ .

A had many enemies
B broke the king's law
C burned a castle
D was the only son of an earl

GO ON TO NEXT PAGE

Name_____   Date _____

Passage III

Play dough is used by children to model interesting animals and objects. Play dough does not have to be bought in a store—children can have fun making their own!

Follow the recipe to see how easy it is to make play dough.

3 cups flour	**1 cup water**
1/4 cup salt	**1 tablespoon vegetable oil**

Mix the salt and flour together. Gradually add oil and water. Mix with hands until dough is well blended. Divide dough into 2 or 3 parts and mix a few drops of food coloring into each part. Store dough in an airtight container for one week.

---

15. The author feels you can make your own play dough because _____ .

A you can't always buy it
B children like to make animals
C it is fun
D it lasts for a week

16. The recipe tells you to _____ .

A mix the dry ingredients first
B add the oil to the salt first
C add food coloring to the flour
D always refrigerate the mixture

17. We can conclude that making play dough _____ .

A is a complicated activity
B uses many ingredients
C is easy for young children
D is too dangerous for young children

18. Young children would probably enjoy making play dough because they like _____ .

A to read recipes
B to mix things with their hands
C the airtight containers
D the different colors

STOP

Suggested Time Limit: 28 minutes   Your time: _____
Check your work if you have time. Wait for instructions from your teacher.

Name_____   Date _____

UNIT VI: MATH CONCEPTS AND COMPUTATION

Lesson 1: Understanding place value, numeration, estimation, and patterns

Part one

DIRECTIONS ▶ For questions 1–3, darken the circle for the correct answer about the place value of numbers. Darken the circle for *E. none* if the correct answer is <u>not</u> <u>given</u>.

 STRATEGY TIPS

1. Read each question twice.
2. Think about which numbers stand for ones, tens, hundreds, and thousands.

Sample:

What is another way to write nine thousand six hundred thirty-seven?

Ⓐ 9,060,37   Ⓑ 9,637   Ⓒ 90,637   Ⓓ 9,603.700   Ⓔ none

ANSWER

The correct answer is *B. 9,637.*

NOW TRY THESE

1. What is another way to write 24 thousands, 3 hundreds, 70 tens, 8 ones?

   Ⓐ 204,378   Ⓑ 240.030,78   Ⓒ 24,378   Ⓓ 2,437,008   Ⓔ none

2. Which of these numbers has a seven in the hundreds place?

   Ⓐ 894,827   Ⓑ 794,123   Ⓒ 894,726   Ⓓ 897,542   Ⓔ none

3. Which of these is 8000 + 600 + 20 + 1?

   Ⓐ 80,621   Ⓑ 806,201   Ⓒ 8,621   Ⓓ 86,201   Ⓔ none

GO ON TO NEXT PAGE

Name_____   Date _____

Lesson 1: Understanding place value, numeration, estimation, and patterns

Part two

DIRECTIONS ▸ For questions 4–6, darken the circle for the correct answer. Darken the circle for *E. none* if the correct answer is <u>not given</u>.

 **STRATEGY TIPS**

1. Read each question carefully to make sure you understand exactly what to do.
2. Study all the choices before you decide on the correct answer.

Sample:

Which of these numbers is greater than the others?

Ⓐ 867   Ⓓ 870
Ⓑ 853   Ⓔ none
Ⓒ 876

 ANSWER

The correct answer is *C. 876*. 876 is greater than any of the other numbers.

NOW TRY THESE

4. Which of these groups of numbers is ordered from least to greatest?

   Ⓐ 116, 97, 89
   Ⓑ 8, 9, 116
   Ⓒ 97, 89, 116
   Ⓓ 89, 116, 97
   Ⓔ none

5. Which of these is a true number sentence?

   Ⓐ 72 < 45   Ⓓ 72 = 45
   Ⓑ 45 > 72   Ⓔ none
   Ⓒ 45 = 72

6. Which of these is the same as DCXXVI?

   Ⓐ 525   Ⓓ 626
   Ⓒ 1521   Ⓔ none
   Ⓑ 621

 GO ON TO NEXT PAGE

Name_____   Date _____

Lesson 1: Understanding place value, numeration, estimation, and patterns

Part three

DIRECTIONS ▶ For questions 7–10, darken the circle for the answer that is the best estimate or nearest round number. Darken the circle for *E. none* if the correct answer is <u>not given</u>.

💡 **STRATEGY TIPS**

1. Round up to the nearest ten if a number ends in 5 or more.
2. Round up if the tens are 50 or more. Do the same if the hundreds are 500 or more.
3. Round numbers when you estimate.
4. Remember that the word *about* means an exact answer is not needed.

Sample:

Round 428 to the nearest hundred.

Ⓐ 400   © 300   Ⓔ none
Ⓑ 500   Ⓓ 450

 ANSWER

The correct answer is *A. 400*. 428 is closer to 400 than to 500, so you do not round up.

✏️ **NOW TRY THESE**

7. Round 526 to the nearest ten.

    Ⓐ 500   © 520   Ⓔ none
    Ⓑ 530   Ⓓ 600

8. Estimate the difference between 81 and 49.

    Ⓐ 30   © 50   Ⓔ none
    Ⓑ 40   Ⓓ 60

9. Estimate the product of 38 x 4.

    Ⓐ 120   © 160   Ⓔ none
    Ⓑ 110   Ⓓ 180

10. Which numbers should you use to estimate 494 + 176?

    Ⓐ 400 + 200   Ⓓ 400 + 100
    Ⓑ 500 + 200   Ⓔ none
    © 500 + 100

GO ON TO NEXT PAGE ▶

Name_____   Date _____

Lesson 1: Understanding place value, numeration, estimation, and patterns

Part four

DIRECTIONS ▶ For questions 11–14, darken the circle of the number that fits the pattern of the other numbers. Darken the circle for *E. none* if the correct answer is <u>not given</u>.

STRATEGY TIPS

1. Study the pattern of the numbers given.
2. Think about a number that would follow the same pattern.

Sample:

What number should come next?

2, 4, 8, 16, ___

Ⓐ 18   Ⓓ 40
Ⓑ 24   Ⓔ none
Ⓒ 36

ANSWER

The correct answer is *E. none*. The pattern for these numbers is to double the number that came before it. None of the answers is the double of 16.

NOW TRY THESE

11. 5,002, _____ , 4,978, 4,966

Ⓐ 5,014   Ⓓ 4,954
Ⓑ 4,990   Ⓔ none
Ⓒ 4,986

12. _____ , 14,346, 14,356, 14,366

Ⓐ 14,316   Ⓓ 14,326
Ⓑ 14,016   Ⓔ none
Ⓒ 14,376

13. 21, _____ , 15, 12, 9

Ⓐ 18   Ⓓ 17
Ⓑ 19   Ⓔ none
Ⓒ 16

14. Which group of numbers is made up of multiples of 3?

Ⓐ 2, 4, 6   Ⓓ 14, 16, 20
Ⓑ 25, 30, 35   Ⓔ none
Ⓒ 18, 21, 24

STOP

Your time: _____

Number right: _____

On this lesson I did _____ because _____

_____ .

Name_____   Date _____

Lesson 2: Practicing whole number computation

DIRECTIONS ▶ For problems 1–14, darken the circle for the correct answer. Darken the circle for *E. none* if the correct answer is <u>not given</u>.

 **STRATEGY TIPS**

1. Check the sign to make sure you are doing the correct operation.
2. Estimate the answer.
3. Cross out any choices that must be wrong.
4. Check your work.

Sample:

307 + 28 + 459

Ⓐ 894   Ⓓ 774
Ⓑ 1,046   Ⓔ none
Ⓒ 794

ANSWER

The correct answer is *C. 794*. You can estimate the sum at about 830. Now you know that the other answers would not be correct.

NOW TRY THESE

1.   78,321
    +   89

Ⓐ 79,400
Ⓑ 78,400
Ⓒ 78,410
Ⓓ 79,369
Ⓔ none

4.   29,630
    − 5,834

Ⓐ 23,794
Ⓑ 23,704
Ⓒ 24,796
Ⓓ 23,796
Ⓔ none

2.   495
      830
    + 185

Ⓐ 1,610
Ⓑ 1,500
Ⓒ 1,510
Ⓓ 1,600
Ⓔ none

5.   572
   x   468

Ⓐ 267,696
Ⓑ 67,696
Ⓒ 20,426
Ⓓ 20,130
Ⓔ none

3. 45 + 29 + 732 =

Ⓐ 716   Ⓓ 706
Ⓑ 806   Ⓔ none
Ⓒ 816

6. 104 x 7 =

Ⓐ 778   Ⓓ 708
Ⓑ 728   Ⓔ none
Ⓒ 828

GO ON TO NEXT PAGE

Name_____   Date _____

Unit 6, lesson 2, page 2

7. $\begin{array}{r} 625,593 \\ -\ 20,948 \\ \hline \end{array}$

Ⓐ 505,848
Ⓑ 514,252
Ⓒ 515,848
Ⓓ 614,848
Ⓔ none

8. $6,409 \div 7 =$

Ⓐ 915 r4
Ⓑ 915
Ⓒ 885 r7
Ⓓ 838 r3
Ⓔ none

9. $39\overline{)1,560}$

Ⓐ 42
Ⓑ 44
Ⓒ 36
Ⓓ 45
Ⓔ none

10. $46\overline{)9,866}$

Ⓐ 206
Ⓑ 184
Ⓒ 214 r22
Ⓓ 214 r12
Ⓔ none

11. Donna's new photo album has 72 pages. If she puts 9 pictures on each page, how many pictures can she put in the entire album?

Ⓐ 650 pictures   Ⓓ 638 pictures
Ⓑ 81 pictures   Ⓔ none
Ⓒ 648 pictures

12. Kelsey is redecorating her room. She bought two throw pillows for $12.47 each and a framed poster for $35.95. How much did she spend in all?

Ⓐ $61.89   Ⓒ $60.89   Ⓔ none
Ⓑ $48.42   Ⓓ $50.42

13. Tammy picked 120 boxes of strawberries last week and earned $85. This week she picked 150 boxes and earned $115. How much did she earn for the two weeks?

Ⓐ $265   Ⓒ $235   Ⓔ none
Ⓑ $205   Ⓓ $200

14. A group of mountain climbers climbed a mountain that was 897 feet above their base camp. Their goal was to reach a mountain that was 9,734 feet high. How many more feet did they have to climb?

Ⓐ 9,631 feet   Ⓓ 8,873 feet
Ⓑ 8,837 feet   Ⓔ none
Ⓒ 9,136 feet

STOP

Your time: _____

Number right: _____

On this lesson I did _____ because _____

_____ .

Name_____ Date _____

Lesson 3: Practicing decimals and fractions
Part one

DIRECTIONS ▶ For problems 1–5, darken the circle for the correct answer. Darken the circle for *E. none* if the correct answer is <u>not given</u>.

 **STRATEGY TIPS**

1. Keep the decimal points lined up when you are doing computation.
2. Remember that you can add a zero to a decimal number without changing its value.
3. Always put a decimal point in the correct place in your answer.

Sample:

4.68	Ⓐ 7.53
+ 2.85	Ⓑ 70.53
	Ⓒ 753
	Ⓓ 75.30
	Ⓔ none

 ANSWER

The correct answer is *A. 7.53.* The other answers either have the decimal point in the wrong place or do not have a decimal point.

NOW TRY THESE

1. 4.622 x 100
   - Ⓐ 462.2
   - Ⓑ 46.22
   - Ⓒ 46.022
   - Ⓓ 4.622
   - Ⓔ none

2. Which number sentence is true?
   - Ⓐ 0.8 < 0.80
   - Ⓑ 0.8 = 0.80
   - Ⓒ 0.8 > 0.80
   - Ⓓ 0.8 = 0.08
   - Ⓔ none

3.
6.27	Ⓐ 2.62
− 3.49	Ⓑ 2.58
	Ⓒ 3.58
	Ⓓ 2.28
	Ⓔ none

4. What is the sum of 0.89 + 2.361 after each decimal is rounded to the nearest whole number?
   - Ⓐ 4
   - Ⓑ 1
   - Ⓒ 3
   - Ⓓ 2
   - Ⓔ none

5. Hugo bought 4 bags of bird seed. Altogether they weighed 36 pounds. If each of the bags weighed the same, how much did each bag weigh?
   - Ⓐ 9 pounds
   - Ⓑ 7.9 pounds
   - Ⓒ 7.6 pounds
   - Ⓓ 9.7 pounds
   - Ⓔ none

 GO ON TO NEXT PAGE

Name_____   Date _____

Lesson 3: Practicing decimals and fractions
Part two

| **DIRECTIONS** ▶ For problems 6–9, darken the circle for the correct answer. Darken the circle for *E. none* if the correct answer is <u>not given</u>.

💡 **STRATEGY TIPS**

1. Remember that a fraction stands for a part of a whole amount.
2. Equivalent fractions name the same amount.
3. Multiply both terms of a fraction by a common factor to find the simplest form of a fraction.

Sample:

Which is the missing number in this set of equivalent fractions?

$\frac{3}{4}$ x $\frac{4}{4}$ = $\frac{}{16}$

   Ⓐ 8
   Ⓑ 10
   Ⓒ 16
   Ⓓ 12
   Ⓔ none

✦ **ANSWER**

The correct answer is *D. 12.* $\frac{12}{16}$ is equivalent to $\frac{3}{4}$ x $\frac{4}{4}$.

✏️ **NOW TRY THESE**

6. What is the lowest term for the answer to $\frac{13}{16} - \frac{5}{16}$?

   Ⓐ $\frac{12}{16}$
   Ⓒ $\frac{3}{8}$
   Ⓔ none

   Ⓑ $\frac{1}{2}$
   Ⓓ $\frac{8}{16}$

7. Which fraction tells what part of the rectangle is shaded?

   Ⓐ $\frac{7}{8}$
   Ⓒ $\frac{6}{8}$
   Ⓔ none

   Ⓑ $\frac{3}{8}$
   Ⓓ $\frac{8}{8}$

8. $\frac{5}{6}$ x $\frac{3}{4}$ =

   Ⓐ $\frac{8}{10}$
   Ⓒ $\frac{2}{20}$
   Ⓔ none

   Ⓑ $\frac{2}{10}$
   Ⓓ $\frac{5}{8}$

9. $4\frac{3}{8}$

  + $2\frac{4}{8}$
  —————

   Ⓐ $6\frac{1}{8}$
   Ⓑ $6\frac{6}{8}$
   Ⓒ $6\frac{7}{8}$
   Ⓓ $6\frac{1}{16}$
   Ⓔ none

🛑 **STOP**

Your time: _____   Number right: _____

On this lesson I did _____ because _____ .

Name_____   Date _____

Lesson 4: Using measurement

DIRECTIONS ▶ Darken the circle for the correct answer. Darken the circle for *E. none* if the correct answer is <u>not given</u>.

💡 **STRATEGY TIPS**

1. Remember that perimeter is the distance around the outside of a figure, area is the measurement of the inside of a figure, and volume is the number of cubic units in a three-dimensional figure.
2. Study the information given about each measurement before you answer the question.

Sample:

What is the perimeter of this rectangle?

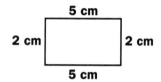

Ⓐ 49 cm   Ⓒ 14 cm   Ⓔ none
Ⓑ 10 cm   Ⓓ 4 cm

ANSWER

The correct answer is *C. 14 cm*. You find the perimeter of a figure by adding the distances around the outside of the figure.

✏️ **NOW TRY THESE**

1. Which digital display tells about the time on this clock?

Ⓐ 4:29
Ⓑ 6:20
Ⓒ 4:22
Ⓓ 6:35
Ⓔ none

2. Which unit of measure would you use to describe the weight of a watermelon?

Ⓐ gram   Ⓒ kilogram   Ⓔ none
Ⓑ liter   Ⓓ centimeter

3. Which unit of measure describes the length of a letter?

Ⓐ feet   Ⓒ yards   Ⓔ none
Ⓑ inches   Ⓓ miles

4. What is the volume of this cube?

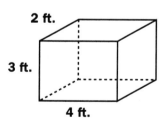

Ⓐ 24 cubic ft.
Ⓑ 9 cubic ft.
Ⓒ 14 cubic ft.
Ⓓ 20 cubic ft.
Ⓔ none

STOP

Your time: _____   Number right: _____

On this lesson I did _____ because _____.

Name_____   Date _____

Lesson 5: Practicing geometry

DIRECTIONS ▶ Darken the circle for the correct answer. Darken the circle for *E. none* if the correct answer is <u>not given</u>.

STRATEGY TIP Study the figures and objects pictured before you answer each question.

Sample:
Which pair of lines is parallel?

Ⓐ   Ⓑ   Ⓒ   Ⓓ   Ⓔ none

ANSWER

The correct answer is *D*. These lines will never intersect.

NOW TRY THESE

1. Which of these figures has a right angle?

    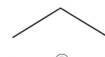

Ⓐ   Ⓑ   Ⓒ   Ⓓ   Ⓔ none

2. Which of these figures shows a line of symmetry?

Ⓐ   Ⓑ   Ⓒ   Ⓓ   Ⓔ none

3. What is the letter name of the radius in this circle?

Ⓐ XZ   Ⓓ YZ
Ⓑ XYZ   Ⓔ none
Ⓒ ZX

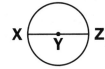

STOP

Your time: _____   Number right: _____

On this lesson I did _____ because _____.

       Test Taking 4, SV 6773-5

Name_____   Date _____

Lesson 6: Using graphs

DIRECTIONS ▶ Darken the circle for the correct answer. Darken the circle for
E. none if the correct answer is <u>not given</u>. Use the graphs.

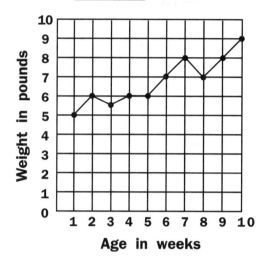

Sample:

The graph shows the growth of Mr. and
Mrs. Tosca's baby. How old was the baby
when he weighed $5\frac{1}{2}$ pounds?

ⓐ 3 weeks   ⓓ 7 weeks
ⓑ 1 week   ⓔ none
ⓒ 5 weeks

The correct answer
is *A. 3 weeks*.

NOW TRY THESE

1. How old was the baby when he
    weighed 8 pounds?

    ⓐ 10 weeks   ⓓ 3 weeks
    ⓑ 6 weeks   ⓔ none
    ⓒ 7 weeks

2. How much did the baby gain
    between 4 weeks and 6 weeks?

    ⓐ 2 pounds   ⓓ 1/2 pound
    ⓑ 1 pound   ⓔ none
    ⓒ 0 pounds

3. In which week did the baby lose $\frac{1}{2}$
    pound?

    ⓐ week 5   ⓓ week 6
    ⓑ week 2   ⓔ none
    ⓒ week 4

4. During which two-week period did
    the baby gain the most weight?

    ⓐ weeks 2–4   ⓓ weeks 4–6
    ⓑ weeks 5–7   ⓔ none
    ⓒ weeks 3–5

Name_____   Date _____

Unit 6, lesson 6, page 2

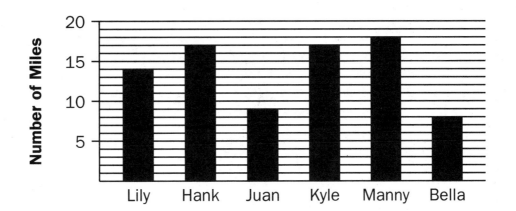

5. Who rode the farthest?

    Ⓐ Bella   Ⓓ Manny
    Ⓑ Hank   Ⓔ None
    Ⓒ Juan

6. How many more miles did Kyle ride than Lily?

    Ⓐ 3 miles   Ⓓ 2 miles
    Ⓑ 6 miles   Ⓔ None
    Ⓒ 1 mile

7. What was the total number of miles that the students rode?

    Ⓐ 100 miles   Ⓓ 95 miles
    Ⓑ 75 miles   Ⓔ None
    Ⓒ 83 miles

8. How many students rode less than 16 miles?

    Ⓐ 2 students   Ⓓ 1 student
    Ⓑ 3 students   Ⓔ None
    Ⓒ 4 students

9. Hank earned $1.15 for each mile he rode. How much money did he earn?

    Ⓐ $25.20   Ⓓ $18.65
    Ⓑ $15.35   Ⓔ None
    Ⓒ $19.55

STOP

Your time: _____

Number right: _____

On this lesson I did _____ because _____

_____.

Name_____   Date _____

PRACTICE TEST 6

Part 1

Directions: For questions 1–4, choose the correct answer. Choose *E. none* if the correct answer is <u>not given</u>. Record your answer on the answer sheet.

Sample: **Which means the same as 1,204?**

    A one thousand two hundred four
    B one thousand two hundred forty
    C one thousand twenty-four
    D twelve thousand forty
    E none

Answer: The correct answer is *A. one thousand two hundred four*.

---

1. **Which number is two thousand six hundred sixty-four?**

    A 2,646   **D** 26,604
    B 2,604   **E** none
    C 2,664

2. **Which of these groups of numbers is ordered from greatest to smallest?**

    A 652, 745, 29   **D** 745, 29, 645
    B 29, 652, 745   **E** none
    C 745, 652, 29

3. **Estimate the sum of 619 + 296.**

    A 900   **D** 890
    B 800   **E** none
    C 920

4. **What number should come next? 18, 24, 36, ____**

    A 37   **D** 48
    B 40   **E** none
    C 44

GO ON TO NEXT PAGE

Name_____   Date _____

Part 2

Directions: For questions 5–8, choose the correct answer. Record your answer on the answer sheet. Choose *E. none* if the correct answer is not given.

Sample: **721 – 356 =**

A 366   D 476
B 365   E none
C 466

Answer: The correct answer is *B. 365.*

---

5.   **5,396**
     +   4,817

A 9,211
B 10,203
C 10,281
D 10,213
E none

6.   **925**
     x   50

A 45,255
B 40,250
C 46,250
D 45,500
E none

7. Chelsea has 55 carnations. She needs to make 5 flower centerpieces for her troop's luncheon. How many carnations should she put in each centerpiece?

A 5 carnations
B 10 carnations
C 12 carnations
D 11 carnations
E none

8. It took 65 minutes for the bus to drive to the amusement park. The class spent 25 minutes at a rest stop. How long did the trip to the park take?

A 85 minutes
B 1 hour and 30 minutes
C 2 hours
D 80 minutes
E none

GO ON TO
NEXT PAGE

Name_____   Date _____

Part 3

Directions: For questions 9–12, choose the correct answer. Record your answer on the answer sheet. Choose *E. none* if the correct answer is <u>not given</u>.

Sample: **Change $2\frac{2}{3}$ into an improper fraction.**

A $\frac{8}{3}$

B $\frac{7}{3}$

C $\frac{5}{2}$

D $\frac{22}{3}$

E none

Answer: The correct answer is A. $\frac{8}{3}$.

---

9. $\frac{5}{8}$

$+\ \frac{3}{16}$

A $\frac{8}{16}$

B $\frac{2}{15}$

C $7\frac{1}{8}$

D $\frac{13}{16}$

E none

10. **Find the difference between $4\frac{7}{24}$ and $3\frac{1}{24}$. Reduce the answer to its lowest terms.**

A $1\frac{6}{24}$

B $7\frac{8}{24}$

C $1\frac{8}{24}$

D $1\frac{1}{4}$

E none

11. **Charlie has $3.00 to spend at the movies. If he buys a drink for $0.78 and popcorn for $1.27, how much money will he have left?**

A $2.05

B $0.95

C $1.05

D $0.85

E none

12. 2.32

– 0.35

A 2.67

B 1.97

C 2.03

D 0.97

E none

GO ON TO NEXT PAGE

Name_____   Date _____

Part 4

Directions: For questions 13–16, choose the correct answer. Record your answer on the answer sheet. Choose *E. none* if the correct answer is <u>not given</u>.

Sample: **What is the volume of a cube that is 10 cm by 10 cm by 10 cm?**

    A 30 cubic centimeters
    B 100 cubic centimeters
    C 300 cubic centimeters
    D 1,000 cubic centimeters
    E none

Answer: The correct answer is *D. 1,000 cubic centimeters.*

---

13. How many angles does this sign have?

    A 4 angles
    B 8 angles
    C 6 angles
    D 10 angles
    E none

14. How many segments does this line have?

    A 1 segment   **D** 3 segments
    B 2 segments   **E** none
    C 0 segments

15. Which is the best estimate of the distance between two cities?

    A 20 km   **D** 20 kg
    B 20 m   **E** none
    C 20 cm

16. Julius and his mom bought hot dogs for the team picnic. About how much did they buy?

    A 8 in.   **D** 8 pt.
    B 8 lb.   **E** none
    C 8 gal.

STOP

Suggested Time Limit: 20 minutes   Your time: _____
Check your work if you have time. Wait for instructions from your teacher.

Name_____   Date _____

UNIT VII: PROBLEM SOLVING

Lesson 1: Practicing with problem solving strategies

DIRECTIONS ▶ Darken the circle for the correct answer. Darken the circle for *E. none* if the correct answer is <u>not given</u>.

💡 STRATEGY TIPS

1. Read each problem carefully.
2. Think about the questions being asked.
3. Decide if there are enough facts to solve the problem.
4. Decide the best way to solve it.

Sample:

Mai is planning to ride her bike to her friend's house. She'll ride five blocks east, turn left and ride eight blocks north, then turn right and ride seven more blocks. How many blocks away does Mai's friend live?

Ⓐ make a list
Ⓑ make a table
Ⓒ make a graph
Ⓓ draw a picture
Ⓔ none

✸ ANSWER

The correct answer is *D. draw a picture.* Drawing a picture is the best way to organize the information to solve the problem.

✏ NOW TRY THESE

1. Mr. Richard's class decides to have a newspaper drive for two weeks. The students will work in teams and give a prize to the team that brings in the most paper each week. How can they find out which is the winning team?

   Ⓐ make a list
   Ⓑ make a graph
   Ⓒ find a pattern
   Ⓓ draw a picture
   Ⓔ none

2. Mattie and Angela's ages together are 22. Angela is twice as old as Mattie. How old is Mattie?

   Ⓐ estimate
   Ⓑ choose the operation
   Ⓒ guess and check
   Ⓓ draw a picture
   Ⓔ none

STOP

Your time: _____   Number right: _____

On this lesson I did _____ because _____ .

Name_____ Date _____

Lesson 2: Practicing problem solving

DIRECTIONS ▶ Darken the circle for the correct answer. Darken the circle for *E. none* if the correct answer is <u>not given</u>.

 **STRATEGY TIP** Solve the problems by using the strategies you practiced in lesson one.

Sample:

Sandy has $10.00. She wants to buy 2 tapes at the music store. The tapes cost $5.53 each. How much more money does she need to buy both tapes?

Ⓐ $2.00   Ⓒ $1.06   Ⓔ none
Ⓑ $11.06   Ⓓ $0.60

ANSWER

The correct answer is *C. $1.06*. To solve the problem, use more than one step. First, add the cost of the two tapes, then subtract $10.00 from the total.

NOW TRY THESE

1. Mrs. Robinson's class is planning a science fair. They will have 24 exhibits on 4 tables. How many exhibits will they have on each table?

   Ⓐ 20 exhibits Ⓒ 28 exhibits Ⓔ none
   Ⓑ 6 exhibits   Ⓓ 16 exhibits

2. Lorna has 21 yards of fabric to make a bedspread and curtains. If she uses 4 yards to make curtains and 13 yards for the bedspread, how many yards of fabric will she have left?

   Ⓐ 17 yards Ⓒ 8 yards Ⓔ none
   Ⓑ 4 yards   Ⓓ 9 yards

3. Sylvia's and Mason's ages together add up to 15. Sylvia is twice as old as Mason. How old is Sylvia? How old is Mason?

   Ⓐ 10, 5 Ⓒ 8, 7   Ⓔ none
   Ⓑ 12, 3 Ⓓ 11, 5

4. Faoud went shopping for his mother. He bought butter for $1.95, oranges for $2.17, and crackers for $1.89. He gave the cashier $10.00. How much change should he get back?

   Ⓐ $3.93 Ⓒ $0.87 Ⓔ none
   Ⓑ $6.07 Ⓓ $4.23

GO ON TO NEXT PAGE

Name_____   Date _____

Unit 7, lesson 2, page 2

5. Donna, Cary, and Brad entered a skating race. In how many different ways could they have come in first, second, and third?

   Ⓐ 12   Ⓒ 3   Ⓔ none
   Ⓑ 9   Ⓓ 6

6. Tony, Andy, and Amy each won a prize in the art show. One won for the best watercolor, one for the best oil painting, and one for the best collage. Andy said, "I like the colors in Tony's watercolor." Amy is a friend of the artist who did the collage. Who did the oil painting?

   Ⓐ Andy   Ⓒ Tony   Ⓔ none
   Ⓑ Amy   Ⓓ a friend

7. The school lunchroom uses 32 pounds of fruit each day. About how many pounds are used in 5 days?

   Ⓐ 150 pounds   Ⓓ 175 pounds
   Ⓑ 200 pounds   Ⓔ none
   Ⓒ 100 pounds

8. Vivian is taking swimming lessons. The first week she swam 8 laps. The second week she swam 12 laps. The third week she swam 16 laps. At this rate, how many laps will she swim in the fourth week?

   Ⓐ 18 laps   Ⓓ 24 laps
   Ⓑ 22 laps   Ⓔ none
   Ⓒ 20 laps

STOP

Your time: _____

Number right: _____

On this lesson I did _____ because _____.

I think it would help me to _____.

Name_____   Date _____

PRACTICE TEST 7

Part 1

Directions: For questions 1–4, choose the best strategy to solve the problem. Choose *E. none* if the answer is <u>not given</u>. Record your answer on the answer sheet.

Sample: The Cupcake Bakery displayed 24 brownies in each of 3 trays. They displayed 16 sugar cookies in 2 other trays. How many brownies were on display altogether?

    A guess and check
    B estimate
    C extra information
    D missing information
    E none

Answer: The correct answer is *C. extra information*. You don't need the information about sugar cookies in order to solve this problem.

---

1. Ms. Casey gave the class 120 math exercises to do. Lenore finished 56 of them at school. How many did she have left to do at home?

    A make a list
    B guess and check
    C use a pattern
    D work backwards
    E none

2. There are 528 seats in the new multiplex movie theater. All of the seats are usually filled 4 days each week. About how many people fill the theater each week?

    A estimate
    B make a graph
    C work backwards
    D more than one step
    E none

3. There are 26 students in Mr. Samuels' fourth grade class. He ordered 21 calendars for each student to sell for a fund raiser. How many calendars did he order in all?

    A write a number sentence
    B make a graph
    C make a table
    D make a list
    E none

4. Derek bought 6 report folders. Each folder cost $0.39. He gave the clerk $3.00. How much change did he receive?

    A make a list
    B extra information
    C more than one step
    D estimate
    E none

Name_____ Date _____

Part 2

Directions: For questions 5–8, choose the correct answer. Choose *E. none* if the answer is <u>not given</u>. Record your answer on the answer sheet.

Sample: Keisha's club made 6 bracelets for Mother's Day gifts. The beads cost a total of $6.65 and the clasps cost $1.15. How much did each bracelet cost?

A $1.10   **D** $ 0.96
B $2.00   **E** none
C $1.30

Answer: The correct answer is *C. $1.30*. To solve this problem, you need to do more than one step.

---

5. Englewood School had a used book drive. They collected enough books to fill 12 cartons. Each carton held 36 books. About how many books did they collect in all?

   A about 300 books
   B about 280 books
   C about 400 books
   D about 600 books
   E none

6. Yvonne works in the school book store. There was a sale on book covers. The sale lasted for 4 weeks. Yvonne sold 122 covers each week. How many covers did she sell?

   A 488 covers
   B 400 covers
   C 800 covers
   D 428 covers
   E none

7. Kevin delivers pizzas for Rose's Pizza House. On Sunday he delivered 9 pizzas. On Monday he delivered 6 pizzas, and on Tuesday he delivered 12 pizzas. How many pizzas did he deliver in the three days?

   A 15 pizzas
   B 18 pizzas
   C 27 pizzas
   D 21 pizzas
   E none

8. There were 18 apples. Six boys shared them equally when they went on a hiking trip. How many apples did each boy eat?

   A 2
   B 5
   C 1
   D 4
   E none

STOP

Suggested Time Limit: 15 minutes   Your time: _____
Check your work if you have time. Wait for instructions from your teacher.

TEST TAKING: GRADE 4
ANSWER KEY

Unit I: Word Analysis
Lesson 1, p. 9
1. D
2. B
3. C
4. B
5. A
6. C

Lesson 2, pp. 10-11
1. B
2. B
3. D
4. B
5. B
6. D
7. C
8. A
9. D
10. C
11. A
12. C

Lesson 3, p. 12
1. B
2. A
3. B
4. B
5. C
6. B

Practice Test 1, pp. 13-15
1. A
2. B
3. C
4. C
5. B
6. A
7. B
8. C
9. D
10. A
11. D
12. B
13. C
14. B
15. D
16. C
17. D
18. D

Unit II: Vocabulary
Lesson 1, p. 16
1. B
2. A
3. B
4. C
5. B
6. D

Lesson 2, p. 17
1. C
2. B
3. A
4. C
5. A
6. C

Lesson 3, p. 18
1. B
2. A
3. D
4. B
5. B
6. C

Lesson 4, p. 19
1. D
2. B
3. C
4. D
5. C
6. A

Lesson 5, pp. 20-21
1. B
2. A
3. D
4. C
5. B
6. D
7. B
8. D
9. C
10. A
11. C
12. C

Practice Test 2, pp. 22-24
1. D
2. B
3. A
4. C
5. C
6. B
7. A
8. C
9. B
10. C
11. D
12. C
13. B
14. B
15. C
16. B
17. C
18. D
19. B
20. A
21. C
22. C

Unit III: Spelling and Language
Lesson 1, pp. 25-26
1. B
2. D
3. C
4. A
5. D
6. A
7. B
8. D

Lesson 2, p. 27
1. D
2. C
3. A
4. C
5. A

Lesson 3, p. 28
1. C
2. D
3. A
4. D
5. A
6. C

Lesson 4, p. 29
1. C
2. D
3. B
4. C

Lesson 5, p. 30
1. B
2. B
3. C
4. B
5. D

Lesson 6, p. 31
1. C
2. B
3. C
4. A
5. D
6. A

Lesson 7, pp. 32-33
1. C
2. B
3. B
4. A

Practice Test 3, pp. 34-39
1. B
2. C
3. B
4. A
5. D
6. B
7. D
8. B
9. C
10. A
11. C
12. A
13. A
14. D
15. B
16. B
17. D
18. A
19. D
20. C
21. D
22. A
23. C
24. B
25. B
26. A
27. B

Unit IV: Study Skills
Lesson 1, pp. 40-41
1. A
2. C
3. B
4. B
5. D
6. B
7. C

Lesson 2, pp. 42-43
1. C
2. D
3. B
4. B
5. C
6. C

Lesson 3, pp. 44-45
1. A
2. C
3. B
4. C
5. B
6. A
7. C
8. B
9. A
10. D

Lesson 4, pp. 46-48
1. A
2. C
3. A
4. B
5. C
6. B
7. A
8. C
9. C
10. A

Practice Test 4, pp. 49-55
1. B
2. C
3. A
4. A
5. C
6. D
7. B
8. C
9. B
10. B
11. A
12. A
13. C
14. B
15. A
16. B
17. A
18. A
19. D
20. C
21. D
22. B
23. C
24. C

Unit V: Reading Comprehension
Lesson 1, pp. 56-57
1. B
2. B
3. B ·
4. A

Lesson 2, pp. 58-59
1. C
2. A
3. D
4. C
5. D

Lesson 3, pp. 60-63
1. C
2. A
3. D
4. D
5. C
6. A
7. A
8. B
9. D
10. D
11. A
12. C

Lesson 4, pp. 64-67
1. C
2. D
3. B
4. B
5. B
6. D
7. C
8. B
9. A
10. D
11. B
12. C

Practice Test 5, pp. 68-73
1. B
2. D
3. A
4. A
5. B
6. B
7. A
8. C
9. D
10. A
11. B
12. D
13. A
14. B
15. C
16. A
17. C
18. B

Unit VI: Math Concepts and Computation
Lesson 1, pp. 74-77
1. C
2. C
3. C
4. B
5. E
6. D
7. B
8. A
9. C
10. B
11. B
12. E
13. A
14. C

Lesson 2, pp. 78-79
1. C
2. C
3. B
4. D
5. A
6. B
7. E
8. A
9. E
10. C
11. C
12. C
13. D
14. B

Lesson 3, pp. 80-81
1. A
2. B
3. E
4. C
5. A
6. B
7. E
8. D
9. C

Lesson 4, p. 82
1. B
2. C
3. B
4. A

Lesson 5, p. 83
1. A
2. A
3. D

Lesson 6, pp. 84-85
1. C
2. B
3. E
4. B
5. D
6. A
7. C
8. B
9. C

Practice Test 6, pp. 86-89
1. C
2. C
3. A
4. E
5. D
6. C
7. D
8. B
9. D
10. D
11. B
12. B
13. B
14. C
15. A
16. B

Unit VII: Problem Solving
Lesson 1, p. 90
1. B
2. C

Lesson 2, pp. 91-92
1. B
2. B
3. A
4. E
5. D
6. B
7. A
8. C

Practice Test 7, pp. 93-94
1. D
2. A
3. A
4. C
5. C
6. A
7. C
8. E

Test Taking 4, SV 6773-5